News from Down to the Cafe

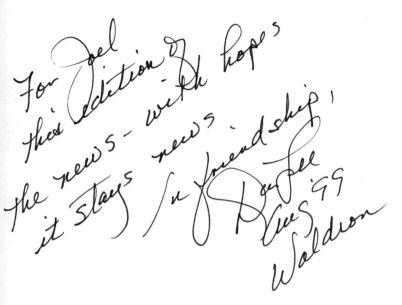

For Joel
this edition of the news — with hopes
it stays news — in friendship,
Dan Lee
Lues '99
Waldron

NEWS
from
DOWN
to the
CAFE

NEW POEMS

David Lee

COPPER CANYON PRESS

Printed in the United States of America.

Special thanks are due to Jim and Judy Swinerton for their generous support of this and other works by David Lee.

Grateful acknowledgment is made to Laura Popenoe for the use of her art on the cover.

The publication of this book was supported by grants from the Lannan Foundation, the National Endowment for the Arts, and the Washington State Arts Commission. Additional support was received from Elliott Bay Book Company, Cynthia Hartwig, and the many members who joined the Friends of Copper Canyon Press campaign. Copper Canyon Press is in residence with Centrum at Fort Worden State Park.

LIBRARY OF CONGRESS CATALOGING-IN-PUBLICATION DATA

Lee, David, 1944–
News from down to the cafe: new poems / by David Lee.
  p. cm.
ISBN 1-55659-132-2 (pbk.: alk. paper)
I. Title.
PS3562.E338 N49 1999
811'.54–DC21

                                 99-6576
                                 CIP

9 8 7 6 5 4 3 2 FIRST PRINTING

COPPER CANYON PRESS
Post Office Box 271
Port Townsend, Washington 98368
www.ccpress.org

For Jon and JoDee, with love

Acknowledgments

The author and publisher wish to express their grateful acknowledgment to the following publications in which poems in this collection originally appeared: *Crab Creek Review, Ellipsis, Fandango, Great Basin Review, Meridian, Midwest Quarterly, Puerto del Sol, Quarterly West, Red Rock Review, Rockville Gazette, Tailwind, Talking River Review, Trask House Broadsides, Wēber Studies, Willow Springs,* and *Witness.* A todos, gracias.

Some of these poems appeared in *Covenants,* Spoon River Poetry Press, co-written with el amigo grande, el jefe Señor William Kloefkorn.

Wayburne Pig was published as a chapbook by Brooding Heron Press, Sam and Sally Green, printers, designers, and loving artists;

The Fish was published as a chapbook by Wood Works Press, Paul Hunter, engraver, designer, printer, sailor, Renaissance man;

The Twenty-One Gun Salute was published as a chapbook by Grey Spider Press, Stern and Faye, printers extraordinaire

– beautiful letterpress artists, all. Abrazos y gracias. You grace the earth with beauty.

Special thanks to Pauline and the home team for both encouragement and demonstration of the patience of Job for putting up with me. Con amor.

To the crew at Copper Canyon, all, blessings. Salud, amor, dinero, y bastante tiempo para gustarlos.

And, of course, Jan who wanders the roads and trails with me. Te quiero.

Contents

News from Down to the Cafe

Wayburne Pig

Cafe where we used to eat was called Wayburne Pig
it wasn't always that but that's how we knew it
it got named that before B.L. Wayburn
beat up Wesley Stevens' new used pickup
with a baseball bat and then
when he come back with his daughter with the big ears
he taken and shot holes in the tires with his pistol
and Red Floyd sed he better retire and move
or they'd have to arrest him and take him to court
even if they didn't blame him one bit
because even before that was when
B.L. Wayburn got them two ugly daughters
of his raised and married
after his third wife run off with a deputy sheriff to Arkansas
and that one boy through highschool
without having to go to the penitentiary
so he sold his cafe and went to farming
sed he was through having to listen to people all day
for the time being and smell grease frying
bought this nice piece of land
spent a backseat full of money
on chainlink fence and concrete floors
for the farrowing sheds
went all over to Missouri he sed to buy
these pureblood Chester White hogs
so he could have the best pigfarm he ever seen
used up all that cafe money
some sed it was because he missed them girls
after they went and left but I didn't think so
or he would of bought Blackshires
with them smashed-up faces
otherns thought he's just putting on airs

some of them pigs cost almost as much money
as God has to be papered hogs
they all guaranteed to not have no disease
and be without worms
he was gone do it right for oncet
and would everbody leave him the hell alone
he was sick and tired of people
and all their humanities
he just wanted to raise hogs by himself

he did good at first without any advice
only lost about all his investment that first year
built his herd up to fifty sows and three boars
he's so proud of those hogs he ordered a sign made
that sed Wayburn's Pigs with a picture of a Chester White
on it to go out by the road in front
but then Wesley Stevens had these two sows come in
it wasn't nothing he'd think of doing
but getting them pigs in there
to one of B.L. Wayburn's papered boars
everbody known Wayburn had sed his place
was closed to all hogs for breeding
and he didn't want to buy any pigs for feeders
he was gone keep all the disease off his land
he wanted a clean herd
so Wesley Stevens loaded those two sows of his up
drove out to his place
in his old Studebaker pickup
right out to the loading chute
with a lock on it so nobody could do just that
he was trying to tear it off
with a tire tool when B.L. Wayburn ran out
sed What in the hell are you doing?
Wesley Stevens sed I brung my hogs

to get bred to your Chestnut White papered boar
get this goddam lock off this loading chute
I haven't got no time to stand here waiting
my hogs is ready right now they slobbering
go get that boar in a hurry

Wesley Stevens' pigs had rhinitis so bad
one's nose was almost looking in its ear
and the other had to eat on one side
of its mouth like its face busted
they were ugly black listed sows
so skinny you could tell
they'd have worms nine foot long
and he fed them dead animals and horses
you wouldn't taste a bite of his sausage
if he offered to pay you five dollars
because you knew the only ones he butchered
were ones that died in their pen
he sold them that lived to Jackson Meat
we didn't eat a whole lot of storebought pig back then

B.L. Wayburn sez Nosir you are not
unloading them two sows on my place
or breeding them to my papered boar
you get in your truck and get off my property
Wesley Stevens put his nose
right in B.L. Wayburn's face sed
What kind of a goddam neighbor are you
you sonofabitch? look in that truck
I done loaded them hogs up all morning
they aint leaving this place till they done bred
and that's a fact
or I'll burn your goddam house down
I won't even wait till night to do it

you don't want to be a good neighbor
you sell out and leave right now
he spit all over B.L. Wayburn's face
mad and hollering like he's deaf in both ears
or was a Mexican who couldn't speak any language
those two hogs so sick with rhinitis
they'd have to stop and rest
walking down an eight-foot loading chute
blowing foam and snot like a bellows
with a hole in the leathers
So what you gone do about it now? he sed
before B.L. Wayburn could even tell him
he'd go call Sheriff Red Floyd by god
Wesley Stevens sed I expected better
of a man that might be my in-law purdy soon

you couldn't have got his attention better
if you'd shot him in the head with a bootlegger's pistol
his mouth flung open
you could have scraped down his eyeballs
with a fingernail file
Wesley Stevens sed That girl of mine's carrying
your grandbaby in her belly right now
so I figger you owe me
till we get them two to the churchhouse
then we'll talk about setting up partners

if you threw a stick on the ground
that daughter of his would have it
before it bounced and be knocked up
she'd already had three kids
and run off a town council
Piggly Wiggly's butcher and a Presbyterian preacher
nobody could have told why any one of them

would come around her
she's so awful looking they sed you'd have to bring
a flour sack to put over her head
even then the front of it would stick to you
where she drooled through
and her ears would poke out on both sides
like it was a mule or milkcow under there
but it was a lie and Wesley Stevens knew it
that boy hadn't been with her since last year
after graduation from highschool
with the football team
we all sed later that might have been too bad
as ugly as those Wayburns were
if them two had kids
we could have closed down the picture show
and saved the money for something to look at
to go with Charley Baker's idiots

B.L. Wayburn ran that cafe so long
he knew how to think and still talk
he sed Look here right now
I've got this one boar I don't need no more
or I'll be using him on his daughters
why don't we just load him up
I'll sell him to you today?
Wesley Stevens sed Is he a papered Chestnut White
I won't have no sorry breeding stock
or no Yorktown hogs on my place
he sed Yas he is I guarantee him for that
Wesley Stevens sez No then I don't believe I can afford him
B.L. Wayburn sed I'll give him to you
Wesley Stevens sez But it cost money to feed him
like the manner he's been custom to
he sed I'll give you 400 pounds of feed to take him

Wesley Stevens sez What about
all my trouble loading up them hogs
and the gas and damages on my truck?
he sez All right
I'll thrown in fifteen dollars cash
that's all I have on me today
Wesley Stevens sez Well if that's the best you can do
so they went and got that Chester White boar
B.L. Wayburn had paid almost 500 dollars for
and loaded it up in Wesley Stevens' Studebaker truck
with 400 pounds of storebought pigfeed
them two sows torn open and ruint
before he even got off Wayburn's place
ascairt that papered boar so bad
they thought he'd climb up those stockracks
to get away but he couldn't
he was stuck for good
Wesley Stevens had what he wanted so he was satisfied
B.L. Wayburn had only one thing to find out
and that was where in the hell
that boy of his was right then

everthing could have been all right
that boy got arrested for breaking in to the highschool
and pouring all the library books on the floor
for something to do on a night
they sed he could go to the army
for three years instead of a trial
B.L. Wayburn thought it was an act of God
he never found out if that Stevens girl
was pregnant to his boy or not
he wouldn't listen to any talk about it
his one ugly girl got divorced with two kids
moved back in and he almost had

the othern's marriage ruint to her husband
when Wesley Stevens brought that boar back
and unloaded him in the hogpasture half a year later

if he'd been kin to you
you couldn't have recognized that pig
he never weighed about half what he did
when he left home that day
looked like a hippopotamuses' head
stuck on a six-foot Viennie sausage
he couldn't even curl his tail up in a knot
Wesley Stevens done bred him
to every hog in the county for fifteen dollars
or a live pig second pick of the litter
he was done worn out for ever
couldn't have got him up on a sow with a comealong
there he stood in that field
with his head down ruint
snorting and blowing blood and snot out of his nose
like he's dying of the pneumonia

that same day his sign for the pigfarm came
man unloaded it by the house and got his money
from that one girl of his living there and left
before they looked at it to see
he'd spelt it all wrong with a *e*
and no *s* on it nowhere
painted a picture of a damn Yorkshire pig on it
with its ears sticking straight up
B.L. Wayburn might as well have been
a Jersey milkcow staring at her first milking machine
at that sign and then that ruint boar
all he could say all morning was
I'll be goddamed

we figured he might have been right that time
put that sign in his garage and shut the door
had to take that boar out and shoot him with his pistol
dug a hole with a tractor and buried him
so the disease wouldn't leak out

it was too late
a year later every hog on his place
had the rhinitis
you could hear them snorting and sucking
like a dry windmill looking for a prime
before you even got out of your truck
took more'n eight months
for the shoats to top out and almost twice the feed
nobody would touch his hogs
if they were looking for sows or feeders to buy
he was as ruint as that dead boar
his girls was so ascairt they went and hid
all the pistol bullets
sed he wouldn't even look out to see the hogs
every day he'd go to the garage
stare at that sign with the wrong pig on the picture
and the words not spelled right
them girls paid the auction to bring four big trucks
haul all the hogs off
sold them to Omaha for sausage at a terrible price
Wesley Stevens made enough
off that boar to buy him a new used pickup
and his girl moved in to town
so she could look for her a husband for those kids

B.L. Wayburn would have probley wasted away and died
except Irby at the bank called him
sed they had to take back that cafe

from those people he sold it to
they couldn't run it worth a damn
and would he be inarrested in a swap back
straight acrost for that hogfarm he bought
since he didn't have nothing to do again
for the time being anyway
and the town needed that cafe to be open

wasn't nothing he could do
but say Yessir without any choice
he had both ugly girls back with him by then
so he'd have them to do the work
while he ran cash register and coffee
till that boy got out of the army
then he could give it to him for a job to do
first thing he did was take and put
a paper in the window that sed
If you even think I might not like you
don't walk through this dam door
signed B.L. Wayburn, owner of this business
then he clumb on top and hung
that sign that was spelled wrong
up on the front of that cafe
with the picture of the Yorktown pig
that we all sed passed a resemblance
to those two daughters of his on it
we knew that was a lie
only one girl in town had big ears
that stuck out like that hog
but we never mentioned it to B.L. Wayburn
we were pretty sure he might have
had his pistol bullets back by then
besides it was just some waiting
till it all would come up to a gusher

we were happy for the time being to have a place
where we could go again for dinner or supper
to find a good hot ham sandwich to eat

The Wayburne Team

Discretion is the greater part of valor.
PLUTARCH

Obsession is the greater part of squalor.
JEFFREY BERKE

Biggest problem we had
setting up the new softball league
was figuring out what to do
about the problem of whores
and what we should say
if the Reverend Coy Stribling
decided he wanted to play

B.L. Wayburn and the widow Wheaton
spent the best part of February and March
thinking up the league and making a schedule
with two teams from Tahoka
sponsored by the cotton gin and the Christian Alliance
made up of the Free Lutherans and Methodists
that believed in the existence of other churchhouses
and two from our town sponsored by
Bill Edwards Hardware and the Wayburne Pig Cafe
with tee shirts and ball hats ordered
and a home and away schedule in writing
starting April for one day a week
and two tournaments on Memorial Day and Juneteenth

called a meeting of the sheriff's deputies
and volunteer fireboys to ask them
if they'd all be on the Wayburn team
as his way to express his thanks

for their community service and sed
he would provide catering for their spring picnic
of soda pop and ham sandwiches
if they would guarantee 100 percent participation
of their organizations on his Wayburn Ball Bruisers
sed Gentlemen this will be a shining moment
in the recreational history of our community
and it wasn't anything they could do but say
that was for sure a fact
sed All the details been worked out
I just need y'alls commitment on this sign-up sheet
I done took care of the rest

R.B. McCravey sed Is it just us or more?
B.L. Wayburn sed What?
Ross Bearden sed Can just anybody play
in this league or only us?
Leonard Askins who was as deaf as a sack of cement
sed What'd he say? both hearing aids
turned up so loud you could hear everything
twice through the earpieces
Ollie McDougald sed We gone be calt the pigs?
B.L. Wayburn sed On my team
Ellis Britton sed Is it wormen gone be allowed?
O'Dean Bloodworth sed It aint no womern
can play softball is it?
Ollie McDougald sed Wormen?
B.L. Wayburn sed What I have in mind
R.B. sed I meant about him and pointed
back to the back booth
where Coy Stribling sat every morning
to eat his early-bird special
of one soft-fried egg and hashbrown arshpotatoes
with two slices of toast and butter and coffee

after looking at the menu for ten minutes every time
with ketchup and jelly and A-1 sauce
and nine refills with cream and sugar for forty-nine cents
while he worked on his Sunday Sermon
listening in while the real people
came to the cafe to have their coffee
and tell each other how it had been
yesterday and back when it was some good times
leaning on his plate like it was a hog trough
Rufus Garner sed Ohlordgod yes
it's some that can play
like they should of been borned men
Billy Shoemaker sed I never seen that before
Leonard Askins sed Seen what?
B.L. Wayburn sed I have this sign-up sheet
R.B. sed If he's on the team
it aint no way I'm gone play no softball
I'd as soon go watch a Jehovah's Witness tent revival

I'll tell you one thing I heard sed Arty Gill
my wife Modean she sed she heard down
to the beauty parlor from somebody
who ought to know over to Tahoka
at the Curl Up and Dye Hair House
they hired this one womern to bend hair
from back East somewhere in Florida
they sed who played softball there
to pay her way through beauty school
and was a professional lady wrestler
can really thrown
that ball named Hazel Wore
on a straight line all the way
from the outfield underhanded home
No kidding? sed Russell Waltrip I never heard of that neither

Never heard what neither? sed Leonard Askins
B.L. Wayburn sed If y'all just sign right here
Bull sed Roy Talbert
that blind sonofabitch Coy
he couldn't hit a pig in the butt with a orningboard
Cephas Bilberry sed No way he caint throw straight enough
to hit him on the same spot with a rock
or a handful of dried-up redbeans
I heard sed Arty Gill she struct out
Leland Haygood's cousin by marriage from second base
and that's a good eighty foot back more or less
on three balls and he never hit close to one
might as well of had his pecker in his hand
or a white salamander as that ball bat
No kidding? sed Ollie you heard that?
No I couldn't sed Leonard Askins not all of it
He sees fine sed Arlis Jamerson
you ast B.L. Wayburn if that aint so
B.L. Wayburn sed Boys just listen
Arlis sed Them glasses he wears
belonged to his wife's daddy before he died
and then didn't need no more
didn't they B.L.? you tell them
Timmons Adam sed I believe
only reason he wears them things
is to look more preacherly
when he goes out in public
Can they put wormen in this league? sed J.L. Biggins

we all stopped talking
and looked at B.L. Wayburn standing
with the pencil and sign-up sheet in his hand
but it was too much pressure to tell the truth
he had to finally whisper That's about it

only reason he wears them specs is to look like he's studying
to show hisself approved before his Lord
rightly dividing words of truth
between them he never heard of before
I caint hear you sed Leonard Askins speak up
I suspicion he keeps them glasses on
so his eyes'll foam up
like a leaky hydrant on a warshing machine
make him look sorrowful and wrenched out
so heg'n quit studying that much sooner
and move to personal meditation
on him and the Lord's many enemies
Is that a fact? Arty sed
Whar? sed Leonard Askins
She was a professional you say? sed Bobby Tippits
Professional what? sed Ollie
B.L. Wayburn sed Coy's wife told
his second wife oncet privately
in confidence not to ever let out
and then she told him one night
old Coy he always hated reading in the first place
starting back before fifth grade even
sed it made his lips too tored
so she had to find a way to help him quit
to put him out of all his misery
now boys about this sign-up
R.B. sed I'd give fifty dollars to
find a way to strangled that sonofabitch
if I could get away with it
From eighty foot off? sed Victor Huffman

it was right then Forest Mason came in
pissed off from being alive
not even drunk looking for a fight to get in

sed What y'all talking about behind my back?
B.L. Wayburn sed It's about the softball league
Arty Gill sed And that womern
over to Tahoka on their team
Coy aint playing sed R.B. and that's that
Whar? sed Forest Mason in Tahoka?
Leonard Askins who was his uncle
and could talk to him any way he wanted to
got right in his face hollered
like nobody else couldn't hear either
They say it's a whorehouse in Tahoka
has a professional womern wrestler working there
can throw eighty miles a hour
Ollie McDougald sed Whorehouse
E.U. Washburn looked up but didn't say anything
Whar in Tahoka? sed Forest Mason
At the ball place sed Leonard Askins
that's what they call it with a whore name Hazel
where she hit three men in the balls
one still crippled and his pecker's incompetent
dribbles down both legs
lays there dead like a white salamander
until it curlt up and died at the whorehouse
that's what I heard
That ain't his pecker leaks all day
sed Goose Landrum that's yours you old deaf fart
See? sed Leonard it's all the truth
just like I told you
In Tahoka? sed Forest Mason
Whore sed Ollie McDougald

We caint have that
in this league sed Shorty Hamilton
I aint playing with no whores or Coy Stribling

sed R.B. and that's my final word
Wormen do not belong on a ballpark
but at home with their chirren sed J.L. Biggins
and no way no professionals
doing bidness out there in front of good people
or my wife if she comes out to see
Whar in Tahoka? sed Forest Mason
Wait a minute sed B.L. Wayburn
CONCABINES and HARLOTS is a abomination
before the Lord hollered Coy Stribling
none of us knowing he was even listening in
back there hunching over his soft-fried egg
with ketchup beat in the yolk looking
like it bled to death before it was cooked
him standing beside his booth
with his napkin tucked in his shirtcollar
I shant offer the support of my flock
to any reckeration offering comfort and solace
to the likes of such while I'm alive
bellowing perfect preacher talk in the cafe
like he was offering prayer over the collection plate

a bowling ball dropped from the water tank
sixty foot down through the ceiling to the coffeecounter
couldn't have interrupted our meditation
on the meaning of hatred and the skankiness
of his presence for about nine seconds
until Ollie McDougald sed Whore?
then R.B. McCravey sed On the other hand
we aint got a right to criticize a womern
for making a living the best she known how
and then Victor Huffman sed I don't see nothing wrong
with allowing any womern on that softball team
as long as she don't deliberately aim

at no men's private parts
B.L. Wayburn sed It's not fast pitch
all balls thrown slow
Arty Gill sed Oh well you should of sed so
Leonard Askins sed Whose balls?
Forest Mason sed Whar's she at?
R.B. sed I make a motion
we allow her to play all she wants to
with any of us she wants to
and all who don't want to
can go find somewhere else to be
we all sed we agreed with that 100 percent
Coy sed I can see me and the Lord is in the upper room
y'all all downstairs with Judast plotting
the filthiness of fornication
I'm gone finish my breakfast and leave
before y'all turn my stomach
I may not ever come back
R.B. sed Mebbe it is a God in heaven
Whore sed Ollie McDougald
Whar? sed Leonard Askins
That's what I want to know sed Forest Mason
It's about this sign-up sheet
sed B.L. Wayburn
I have to get all the names wrote down
now before he changes his mind
we caint get started till I have
all the names on this paper for the team

Rhapsody for the Good Night:
Christmas Eve

1

Libations
liquid and flowing
beneath the knees of the gods

Strangest man ever was E.U. Washburn
his Bible name was Ethiopian Eunuch
came from that family opened the book
whatall was there got named
had Cephas Peter that we called C.P. or Junior
and hated because he went to school studying typewriter
came back educated where he knew
the meaning of life and wrote it in a four-page paper
for the college
loved to tell about it but never got the idea
wasn't anybody listening
the other brother Phillip Chariot
we called Bubber because he had his harelip
so he watched television until Floyd Scott
got fired at Christenson's Brothers
they hired Bubber to make coffee and clean office
nurse tried to not let them name him that
but Dr. Tubbs sed go ahead
they'll call him by the letters anyway
they did so E.U. worked at the graveyard
digging and tending with Jesus Salinas

he's the baby so they raised him with Bubber
probley not talking a whole lot

when he's grown up most people or some
never knew he could say anything at all
some sed he was deaf and dumb
addled but they's wrong all three ways
he mostly didn't like to talk
he'd come to the cafe by himself
sit and listen and nod

oncet it wasn't any place open to be with people
I went back to where he was in the booth
sed E.U. can I set here with you drinking coffee?
looked at me but I never sat down till he nod
sed How y'all anyway? he lipped Justfine
first time I heard him say anything
when we were through not saying anything
for a half hour listening to the otherns
I sed I gotta go you need a ride?
I had to drive past the graveyard to the farm
he never sed anything then either
got up paid his bill
went out got in my truck
both of us drove to work that way
for more'n a year till I got a job
at the sawmill and had to leave early

he talked soft
couldn't play the radio to hear him
when he sed something at all

sed Them's the hardest that day when I sez
It's bad about that Reuben Jimenez boy
who was in the Boy Scouts until he
died of the appendicitis when he's fourteen in highschool
on the operating table without waking up

it was a month later before he sed more
that was what opened the gate
sed That boy isn't figured out he's gone yet
I dunno what to do about it
they buriet him in the wrong place
isn't nobody there to help him or tell him what to do
I sez Whar?
didn't have any idea what he's talking about
he sed That Jimenez boy
longest speech he'd sed up to then
I had to think for almost a week
couldn't make it add I sez How do you know? then
without asking What? he sed
I can tell

2

nightbird
and the hum of pickup tires on hardscrabble

I listen
behind the mockingbird behind the wind
behind the sound a taproot makes
working its way down to water
past that I can hear them
theyg'n hear me too
if they want to
but they mostly don't
sometimes I talk
not to them mostly
to myself to the wind
to the field mouse under the plastic grass
in the shed by the mesquite tree
sometimes they pay attention
it's other ways too
like how they settle in to stay
or don't

Leona Huffington there
has her back to her husband
won't talk to him
but doesn't even know
he don't care

Baucis and Philemon Rojas had both
sed look for a bright spring sunrise they'd be
in bed sleeping in their morning garden
next to each other past tomorrow's dawn
Jesus thought the one plot was fine with the
headstone with one name but both in the one
red box under a blanket dressed that way
he wasn't sure of but they'd planned it through
it was what they wore their first night they wrote
so Rufus did just like they said then we
planted on both sides of their place the two
rose stalks they'd raised by their garden window
roses bloom now over the stone in a
bow bright red as Easter-morning sunshine

that other rosebush over there by Tommy Malouf
it's growing right out the palm of his hand
and in that flowerplant it's a mockingbird every day
pointing itself right at
Janie Grace Gosset who got killed
in the car wreck in highschool singing
aint never a weed grown at her place
that Malouf boy give her flowers and the song
she settled right in knowing she belonged

some out there's helpless
like that Reverent Brother Strayhan
found out it aint at all

24

like what he been told to think
now it's too late
biggest surprises
was Ellis Britton and Kay Stokes
everbody thought Ellis he wouldn't never
fit in cause he's so mean
he was the happiest I ever seen
found out we's all wrong
he never hated the people
he hated the living
Mistah Stokes now on the other hand
he hated us all
so he aint never settled in
probley won't at least as long as Jesus is watching
can't get used to not being in charge

on a night of a full moon that comes on a payday
I seen Jesus out there with him getting drunk
telling him about all the times he come
thrown him and his family off the No Lazy S
sworn at him in front of his chirren and dog
now he sez Well now Mr. Kay Stokes I believe
I'll go fishing down to the tank by the blue gate
catch me that big catfish they say down there
so what you think about that Mr. Kay Stokes dead man?

I'll swear I seen
one thousand dandelion weeds pop up
all over that grave in a night
when he's been listening to Jesus
whole grave come up three inches
he's trying so hard to get out
I rakes him back down in the morning sunshine

Ellis Britton settled
in two weeks or a month
so fast we never paid it mind
when the otherns out there saw he's ready
they started the rumor
we all have to come back do this all over again
he slunk down deep and low as he could
holding on tight
took two wheelbarrows to level him up
he just fine
a satisfied mind

3

Music is silence.
The reason we have the notes
is to emphasize the silence.

DIZZY GILLESPIE

owl say Who
preacher say Whar
Rufus say Here
me and Jesus
we start building
a hole in the ground
he sing
Lead me gently home Father

dying
crying
singing
preaching
praying
bringing
burying

then we all begin
the next beginning
covering
forgetting
remembering
calling
neglecting
loving
hating
moving on along

out here
back there
all the same:
wind blow
bird sing
grass grow
churchbell ring

nighttime quiet
it all sink in

4

romantic interlude
of a windy afternoon:
sunlight and elmshadow on stone

year later Christmastime
I saw E.U. of a morning sed Set down
we drank coffee till the otherns left
he sed I got that Jimenez boy settled
I sez You did? he sed Yas
but it almost costed me the farm

Wasn't nobody hepping
they done forgot about him
all alone and scairt
down there whar it aint no time
I had to extablish a reason
they had to hep him in

I known if I could get Mistah Kay Stokes
working against my case
they'd all the rest hep that boy
I sed Aint we all from the same clay?
he sed Mebbe that's so boy
but it aint no jug is a vase

I sed Does a man
have to come down there early
to set that boy to rest at home
cause if you aint gone do it
then I'll have to
Jesus'll clean your yard alone

that's whatall it took
Ruby Patrick sed to her own daddy
Neither one's porcelain so there you go
Janie Grace Gosset sed Whar's that boy?
Tommy Malouf sed I'll find him
mockingbird flown to the Rojas rose

it was a whispering in the grass
in the trees in the wind Whar? sed Ellis
Whar's he at whar's he at? they sed *¿Dónde dónde?*
mockingbird took him the song
in words he could understand
in a day the prodigal son he come home

5

in his hand a glass
filled with the moon
        drowned in branchwater
or
what E.U. said
on Christmas Day

Here's to the newyear
and here's to the old one
and here's to the place in between
the sunrise and the morning
between the midnight and the fullmoon
that place
between the owlcall and the mockingbird
between the roostercrow and the last henlight
under the trees under the rose
under the grass under the shadow of a footprint
that place
where all the naming and the doing
where all the listening and talking
where all the lying and the truesaying
where all the storying and the singing
where all the words theyselves
which is the first and last thing of all
slide into quiet
that dark sleeping place they can call home
just between the dreamsay
and the realsay of it all
that place
where those who know
who live there
know that without the making and remembering and telling
to help us all get on along
it aint no difference or worth finally
in none of it at all

Sonora Portable Music Master
(Made in the United States of America)
55 to 500 Kilocycles Table Model

*Based on an urban folktale told to me by the
honorable John Henry, Sculptor Laureate of
Miami, Florida, and containing technical
information supplied by the honorable
William Kloefkorn, Poet Laureate of
Nebraska, master tellers of tales, both.*

1

Winnie Mae Williamson sed out loud
she didn't necessarily blame the Lord
one bit personally for her getting old alone
without anybody there to help her out
but it didn't seem fair
not to have one thing her own property
even a radio after all them years
waiting for it to happen
started bawling so she couldn't
even finish her dinner
they had to take her back to her room
at the Iron County Rest Home all afternoon
alone resting and waiting
wouldn't even come down to supper
squalling for the injustice of it all

the Lord must have seen and had a vision
sent it to a fatnurse named Colleen
who came to B.L. Wayburn and told him
he sed he didn't see any way he could
help out personally not being
professionally connected or otherwise
to the old-folks' home but she should tell

of her own accord the Lord's message
to either Brother Coy Stribling or better
the Reverend Brother Strayhan
so she did exactly that

Reverend called an unannounced special Wednesday night
fasting and offering session of the Baptist prayer meeting
locked the churchhouse doors
after they were all in and sat down
sed Brethern and sisteren
we have the problem of an unfortunate lostsheep
from our fold living shorn of her youth and forsaken
alone and forgotten without even the comfort
and succor of the gospel brought to her
with the convenience and divers necessity
of the modern technology as our poor
sister-in-Christ Williams has not so much
as even a radio in her loneliness to grant her solace
in the closing hours of her striven and wonderous life
and the Lord has given it us to beseech
on bended knee a remedy for her great need
who will now lead us in this sweet hour of prayah?

all the elders and deacons lined up
to see who could be first and last
wormen sniffling and children reading the songbooks
for about six until Victor Huffman
after Lee Bowen prayed on
for fourteen minutes and forty-two seconds on his turn
with Arlis Jamerson waiting to be next
stood up sed he would make the sacrifice
of offering a radio from Huffman Furniture Store
at his cost plus ten percent more or less
he'd pass the collection plate himself

and help count the money to see if it was enough
but it wasn't the Reverend sed
they'd have to go again he supposed
him set to start another round
with Brother Jamerson standing before the Lord
to be next already moving his lips practicing
held up his hand for the Lord
to bend his ear and listen but Ellis Britton sed first
We aint looking to buy her no Victrola
check and see if it's enough there
for something cheaper of plastic
she's old it won't have to last that long
just one that works with a hard top
so them people there can't drool in the works
leaning over to fool with the dials
changing all the stations
some people don't have all night
to be locked up in a churchhouse waiting
my wife made redbeans for supper
we gone need to be moving round
soon of the pressure
so Victor Huffman who was sitting
right in front of the Brittons
sed him and the Lord could provide
a good medium quality grade Philco
or model of a similar brand name reasonably priced
for about what they had give or take
he prayed without asking permission the benediction
no closing hymn or offering of the invitation
wasn't anything the Reverend could do
but unlock the door and let his sheep
out of their folds loose upon the world

2

Month later the Reverend Strayhan and Victor Huffman
elders and deacons with Ellis Britton
and B.L. Wayburn went to the nursing home
to visit Mizrez Williamson
stood like a halo around her bed
that radio on her table
with its three knobs and wooden slat speaker covers
concave front to spread and harmonize the sound
playing gospel hymns from Harding College
her so proud she sat right up
sed Praise Jesus and thank you Lord
for these fine men brought me
this music from the House of the Lord
that nurse who was her niece
sed it was nothing short of a miracle
told them her appetite
came back just fine
eight years been returned to her youth
since that great gift from the prayer meeting
come into her life
they were all proud of them
for the sacrifice and inspiration

Oh yes sed Winnie Mae
you caint imagine the loneliness
my roommate here for the last six years
Arlene Bloodworth Lucille's grandmother
by marriage before they converted to Pentecostal
ninety-three years old this month
five years and six days more than me
with her own radio all that time
never once let me pick the station
even when Joe Bob Trammel

come in with the tent meeting revival
put him all on the air
she wouldn't budge from her program
now praise Jesus I listen
to whatall I want to hear
the Lord's glorious music and word
with thanks to you fine brethern
here in my own room

sed Oh last week it was a tragedy
Arlene getting up to go to the bathroom
tripped on her houseshoes
because they all worn out
and it's too early for Christmas
fell and knocked her radio on the floor
it's all busted and ruined
they thought at first she might of broke her hip
set on her bed and cried and cried
then on Saturday night asked me
if she could play my radio
on her own favorite program
I could look her in the eye
after six years I told her
Fuck you you old Nazarene bitch
they moved her into another room
now I have all my privacy

3

wasn't nothing they could say
Reverend Strayhan had to try three times
to get the prayer offered
first time *Now I lay me*
second *Bless this food which*
finally sed Oh Lord

watch over thy lostsheep
and bless the churchhouse and its minister
of the Lord to prosperity
they all sed amen and left
she never turned down the gospelsinging
even for her private churchhouse blessing
she was so satisfied with it all

Ellis Britton outside
was the only one to add it up
when they all stood there
scraping their feet on the sidewalk
sed he never blamed her one minute
it was hers to do what she wanted with
and all them Nazarenes could
go straight to hell
as far as him and Jesus cared one bit

then they all went in their cars
home for supper
except Ellis who rode with B.L. Wayburn
back down to the cafe
humming "Leaning on the Everlasting Arms"
all the way

Labor

NEHEMIAH 6:3

ECCLESIASTES 9:10

Harold Rushing died
so we had to change the way
we talked about him

they took and gave the sorriest funeral
I ever saw for his wife Suetta to listen to
him looking terrible in his box on a Thursday
the sun shining outside while that preacher
went on about the glories of the churchhouse
and the love of the Lord for the collection plate
never sed anything about
how that man would rather farm than eat
the week's work he'd try to get done
in a day when he didn't have to be embarrassed
in there laying down
in front of people
with a damn necktie on

I've seen him of a summer
on a tractor holding his dinner
in a bucket and a waterjug in a towsack
hanging on the fender in his other hand
seven Butterfingers in his shirt pocket
thirty-six hours without any sleep
six and a half days on a week
till he had to drive up to town
to be a Campbellite elder on Sundays
where he could get some rest
if they didn't ask him to offer prayer

he broke his arm on a power takeoff
this hired hand had to get his wife
to call Doc Kitchens to come out to the north field
to set that bone
he sed he didn't have no time to wait
kept on working with his hand
flopping like a blue flag on his wrist
with his handkerchief wrapped around
so he wouldn't have to look at it
Doc Kitchens had to go out there
and he had a horrible time catching him
on his tractor because he'd been drinking whiskey
it was a Saturday
and he didn't have any appointments
for breaking bones that day
Harold Rushing stopped working long enough
so he could tie it in a splint with doctor tape
Doc Kitchens sed Let's go to town
put that all in a cast with the X ray
he sed Not today I have work to do
I'll bring it in right before churchtime tomorrow
Doc Kitchens sed Only if you come to the office
I aint putting it on
in the churchhouse parking lot

wasn't a week later changing
sucker rod on that windmill
out to the east gate by the pasture
with the cast on when the wind came up alone
threw him off on the othern
where the bone stuck through
both arms ruint then
back on that tractor next morning
sed Suetta and the hired hands would have to:
Carry buckets

Shovel
Hammer nails
Pick up eggs
and Milk cows
but he could do the rest
they'd have to get by with the inconvenience

had his first heart attack
when he's about fifty-six years old more or less
Doc Kitchens sed Harold Rushing
you got to slow down
let them hired hands do more of that heavy work
you're posta be paying them to do
or that heart's gone give up on you
you got to start treating things better
Harold Rushing sed It lives with me
it'll have to keep up best it can
Doc Kitchens sed You haven't learned
one thing for being alive have you?
he sed Yessir Doc Kitchens I have
I learnt if I walk slow through that door
on the way out of here and it's swinging
it'll bump me on the butt
and that aint gone happen today
I'll see you after the sermon on a Sunday
so you can get your sins and equity paid up
brang me the bill and I'll pay it then
if I don't have to listen to no more today

he died when he's sixty-two
in his field bucking bales with an eighteen-year-old
hired hand driving truck for wages
of a heart attack that Doc Kitchens
sed was such a stroke it could of busted in two

he tore the front of his shirt off
beat bruises and knuckle spots
all on his chest where he tried to get to it
they sed he'd of strangled that heart to death
if he could of got his hands on it
but it wasn't enough time left to break through
Harold Rushing didn't have any use for nothing
that tried to quit before the work got done
on a day when the Lord's sun was shining

Blow

I expect the town will still be talking
about the big fight between
Forest Mason and Billy Shoemaker
into the next century
if we decide we still want to have one

they were the two toughest boys we had
legends of scrapping in their own minds
we all knew it was only time
till they had to settle it down
who was the most worthless dumbass fool
between the both of them
it all came to a head
on a hot evening with the sun still up
of a June on Main Street
in front of the pictureshow
half the town already coming
to buy tickets and go see whatever it was showing
almost the rest got there
soon as they heard those two
were set to have a go at it
Johnny Hopkins sed he wished he could of moved
it inside the showhouse and sold tickets
three weeks in advance
he could of paid off the farm

people got excited
when Forest Mason took off his shirt

sed he didn't want it tore or none
of Billy Shoemaker's blood on it
when he mashed up his face
Billy never took his off
it had buttons up the front
we weren't sure he'd figured out how they worked
we were mostly worried he wouldn't
bite his tongue off hanging out
and choke on it if he got hit
whole crowd milling in a circle
like all the animals in the barnyard
around two boar hogs blowing snot and shouldering
calves with their tails up in the air
and then when the hogs smash together
it's a bawl and green cowshit everywhere
when they break and run
people elbowing and pushing to get up
close enough to see what might happen
as excited as a banshee
trying to windowpeep in an old-folks' home
Coy Stribling with this year's blue Gideon Newtestament
in his hand in the street hollering
Whoso raiseth his hand against his neighbor
is worse than a infidel
R.B. McCravey sed If you don't shut that up
I'm gone whup you better'n I did
in the fifth grade whyn't you go on home?

them two closing in Forest telling Billy
whatall he was getting ready to do to him
like a preacher or insurance salesman
Billy concentrating so hard
he went cross-eyed trying not
to get his feet tangled up circling

then one of them swung out
like a canoe paddle but didn't hit anything
othern was a billygoat coming in with his head down
then they're on the ground wallering
old George Albany who went blind fighting
in the boxing ring standing there listening
with his pencil drawer around his neck coaching
hollering Wake to the belly
wake the belly and the head'll fall
lefhook down low's it'll go up
Billy Shoemaker jumped up
grabbed Forest Mason by the leg
jerked off his boot and flung it
up in the air, whole crowd of people
yelled like wet flags at a football game
most couldn't even see which one it was
hollered By god that's some fighting now
neither one with as much as a knuckle scratch

then it was a miracle
like every god in the universe
came to shove in and watch
clouds all around in about a minute turned black
boiled up like a pot of redbeans ready to spill over
and blow the spigot off the pressure cooker
Coy got to the part hollering
Behold the handiwork of the Lord
standing on the fender of his car
so he could see
it was a piece of lightning struct
wrapped up in a fistful of thunder
like the Potts coalmine blowup
in a bunch at the same time
we all thought we'd been killed

it was so close
whole crowd tried to break and run
whichever direction it wasn't standing
a mountainlion come down in the hogyard
or a giant eggbeater couldn't have torn them up so much
knocking each other down
stepping on their heads and backs and private parts
old George Albany hollering Give them room
give them room to fight
eight people had to go to the hospital
one with its arm out of socket at the elbow and wrist
Forest Mason got stomped so bad
it broke his leg in two places
him yelling at Billy By god
I never brung my friends to help out
except one little boy standing there
still as the quiet spot in the eye of a hurricane storm
eating an ice-cream cone eight years old
named Jimmy Jack Field
never missed a lick on his dessert
his feet stuck like 16-penny nails in the street
his whole mind turned only to chocolate ice cream

it was Coy's one true God's finger descending
tornado came down out that cloud
with the crazywomern scream of an airplane
coming down like a blind hawk on an empty paint can
for a head smashing
with an eighty-car Burlington freight train
brakes locked and squalling as it came in on
a diesel rig stuck on the track
airhorns bellowing like the firealarm
at the end of the world

three times that tornado came down
tore into the ground in the same place
in a vacant lot a block off Main Street
tried to dig in like a railroad spike
made out of wind just across the road
from Charley Baker's junkyard
his idiot boy sitting there playing with matches
and a can of gas
probably never heard a thing
jumped off and went to find
another part of town where it waded
into four houses and a barn
killed one black man we never knew by name
and carried off one of Wesley Stevens' sorry sows
he sed was going to have twelve pureblood pigs in a week
disappeared right up in that cloud
Coy Stribling still on that car fender preaching
his wife sed Coy it's a tornader
he sed What? she sed Well look Coy
he sed Godomitey
I never saw him run so fast

huge rain come like in buckets pourn
or gulleys after a cloudburst on the caprock
and you're wandering trying to find a way
to the top and here it comes down
a frogstrangling clodbuster on you
washing you elbows and legs over armpits to Two Draw
or an ant right there on top when a cow
pees on a flat sandstone rock
then fire in the middle of the rain
burnt down three houses and the streets blocked off
where the firetrucks couldn't come to that end of town
and hail like all the gods gone crazy

some of it as big as gooseeggs
thrown through carwindows and garageroofs
chased down four sheep in Morris Dannelly's forty-acre field
busted their heads flat on the ground
all in a bunch braided up
like somebody beating you with a wet rope
took off straight west to Tahoka
old Clarence Benson fishing without permission
on No Lazy S by the red gate
sed with his own eyes he seen
that cyclome come down
torn a hole in that tank where you could see
the bottom of it naked
two fish laying there so suprised
they couldn't even flop
then lifted up and gone
never even bothered his line

horrible horrible
town twisted up in knots
I saw where wind drove a stem of straw
through a plate-glass window till it stuck
halfway out and a piece of barbwire
into a goat's head and it lived
hanging out one side
almost everybody in the flats got hit
shantyhouses smashed around
like a giant shrike came down
all they owned strung out with the
mouses or toads or little birds
it'd caught and hung wiggling on the thorns
in the mesquite trees or even on the fence barbs
and in the quiet after the cloud was gone
us still there with the hurt and pain

shrike sits on a telephone wire
and trills calling for rain

in a week we had that stormcloud
up to 400 feet across
sound like the bugles of judgment day
and the fight had ballbats and knives and chains
Billy Shoemaker almost died when
Forest Mason hit him over the head
with an eight-foot board and then a roller skate
but Billy jumped up and grapt his leg
broke it in up to nine places
when he jerked it like a snapjointed babydoll
or stomped it on the curb or thrown him
under a passing Greyhound bus
and Wesley Stevens sued Bryant Williamson
and the insurance for 800 dollars
for his prize almost-registered Chestnut White hog
and all the breedingstock in her
he lost for four generations the night of the storm

tourists even come to see the site
where it all took place
in a month half the town
seven dogs and eighteen sheep
four cows and a mule and one cat
crushed by the tornadocloud
one man killed and two maimed in the fight
which was between a man and his son
or over a blindwomern scorned or
a pregnant girl by her brother and cousin
or the killing of a Spotted Poland China hog
and where was it at? the treelimb
stuck through the picture window

growing without a crack and the man living
with two foot of fencewore
hanging out the side of his head
and through his eye every inch a kink
all in a wad where even we
couldn't tell which one we were talking about
Forest with his leg doctoring and Billy
like Siamese twins taking all the credit
for putting the town on the state map
being dumb enough to try and bust his hand
on somebody else's head who was dumber
to put it in the way
like grown men have been doing for 10,000 years
sitting in the cafe bragging
about how terrifying it all looked
two crowing magnum monkeymen
out of a seventh-grade biology schoolbook

then the preachers had to tell us what it all meant
Reverend Strayhan sed It was
the invisible God come with a warning
Ollie McDougald stood up and paid his bill
sed You Baptists don't know doodley-squat
I was there and seen it myself with my eyes
plain as the coffee in your cup
Billy Bob Jackson a month later came in
sed The whole town got baptized by that storm
Coy Stribling heard and in a sermon sed
That was a lie bitter as gall
Jesuschrist he never heard of no showerbath
to be warshed in the blood of the lamb
it had to be total nursing
or none of it never

never never never never
didn't signify one thing at all

years later drinking coffee
we still didn't know
whatall any of it could mean or be
Forest Mason was dead of a heart attack
Billy Shoemaker was being the highway patrol
the clock had moved on
so had we
nobody knew which
marked the time of which
we put up a stone
on the dead man's grave
sed S.K. Blackman for storm killed
E.U. had flowers blooming
all along the way
R.B. sed his only regret
was that he didn't kill him
during the stampede
when nobody could of told
but we figured Coy for once
might of been right
we were all damned souls
fighting in the wind
shorn bawling lambs in the storm
lost from the fold

Song E.U. Washburn Heard Sung
to Tommy Malouf from the
Cummings Plot

I remember a red covered bridge
and a yellow-and-black butterfly,
evening and a nighthawk
over moving water.
Her words turning the world
called the moon
like a great stone pulled up
from the earth and broken away,
its taproot sliding back soft
into the mountain's belly
while the white child
wandered like the lost thing I became
alone in the twilight sky.

I put a buckle
on that moon and the sound
of her voice hanging in the air,
held it in my hand
one with the night
until a cloud covered me
and the moon climbed into dream,
words swallowing us
like a gush of cold mountain water.
When we had been
all was unchanged where we had gone:
moonlight, bridge, dustmotes,
butterfly, river, the nightjar's song.

Sonata in Red

"On a field, Sable, the letter A, Gules."
NATHANIEL HAWTHORNE, *The Scarlet Letter*

Timmons Adam was upwards
of sixty-eight years old retired
from being a teller at J.R. Potts bank
when he came in the cafe
the first time alone
after living in town his whole life

he and his wife were married
long enough they both knew
they didn't like each other
also knew there wasn't anything
they could do to do
anything about it
so they waited it out

she kept a short leash
we figured she figured
if she didn't want anything
to do with him
nobody else could either
watched a lot of TV

it was a miracle
she died first
he buried her in her own
family plot
opened up all the curtains
let some air
blow in the house

Boys he sed the minute he walked in
it's a A for Adam red-letter day
I done read the will
believe I inherited
my own family estate
gentlemen the drinks are on me
we all got a fresh cup
of coffee that day

came from then on
almost the rest of his life
right out of bed
for coffee and breakfast
smiling like the sunshine
down to the cafe
wearing a black suitcoat and bow tie
mostly bright red
about every single day

Burn

Morning coffee
B.L. Wayburn sez You boys
hear about that fire last night?
nobody else in the cafe yet to talk to
me and E.U. sat at the counter
I say I seen but I was too tored
to go start the car and look
E.U. nod, I say who was it?
B.L. Wayburn sez Old Wheaton place
burnt to the ground slap down
I say Was the widow Mizrez Wheaton hurt any?
B.L. Wayburn sez No she wasn't even there
but her and me both know
who burnt that house down for a fact
I say Isatso? he sez Yas
and I can tell you two on a oath
it was Henry Wheaton
E.U. sed Say what?
he's been tending his place
at the graveyard for over a year
that was almost the first time
he ever sed anything out loud
and the longest speech he'd made
inside of the cafe sitting there

I guess you boys done heard
how she been feeling his presence
in that house for some time now
B.L. Wayburn sez She sed
it was like how when somebody just died
you can feel this thing

she don't know another word for it
she just call it Death in the house
every room you go in to
it come to her a while ago thinking
she known it was him stalking
wandering trying to find his way back

sed every time she went to go in a room
you could feel him right there
push by her like a dog
trying to get ahead
to get in there and see what it is
you're looking for
before you find it yourself

and that whisper in the walls
under the floor
like it's talking about you
that you caint quite hear
when she stop to listen
hold her breath in
to see if it would call out her name
it quits or almost seems
like it's crying or laughing quiet
like it could of had its hand
over its mouth
to half hush the tormenting
I done told her more'n twicet
to sell that farm
and get on with her life

E.U. and I known that was true
the real estate listed it up
for half a year but was nobody

interested in that beat-up place
Henry Wheaton sold his crop for birdseed
every year after the weeds
took over the fields
till the soilbank came in and the government
paid him that much to not plant anything
just get out of the way and let them grow
it was one careless weed
they put on the radio got so big
if we would have found a way to keep it green
we'd prop it up by the courthouse
and decorate it for the county Christmas tree
it would've took a man
with twelve kids and a bullwhip
four years day and night
to clean that land up to where
you could even get horse hay to make
and that house would have been proud to say
the taste of paint had never crossed its lips
since the day Henry Wheaton moved in
only man in the state who'd sell him insurance
was Bryant Williamson and then
not for crops or hail or wind or roof
or liability on the porch and floor
if somebody fell through
who might kill himself and break his leg
even Ellis Britton sed that farm was such a damn mess
he might as well give it to the churchhouse
and hope for credit down the road with the Lord
but before that could happen
Henry Wheaton got sick and died

B.L. Wayburn sez She sed
she could feel it coming to a knot
when she set down on the furniture

in the kitchen yesterday evening
sed out loud Henry
I want you to hear me out
I been a widow in mourning
for long enough now
it's time I make a change
time I follow good advice
time I get on with my life
and that mebbe means finding a man
who'll take me for his new wife

sed that house went as quiet
as the sound of Elmer's glue drying
and as cold as the inside
of a married Republican womern's heart
then it was like all the wind
in the world's inside that kitchen room
wrapped up in a bunch
curtains stuck to the window screens
and don't know how to get out
she sed it got so heavy
the inside of that house
weighed more'n the moon

ascairt her so bad
she run right out the back
let the screendoor slam shut
on her way to the car
got out in it when she turnt the key
it was like a evil spirit had his hands
in the starter pulling back the brushes
and the othern froze the solenoid
dead as a smashed cat
at the bottom of a grain elevator shaft
wouldn't crunk

she was terrified till she thought
her hair might be going white
sed sweat like great drops of blood
come up and appeared on her flesh
it was like a vision from the Lord
when she remembered the words to say
hollered In the name of the Father
and the Son and the Holyghost
you go on and get behind me
out of here you sonofabitch right now
sed that car started without touching the key again
brake come off by itself
all she had to do was put it in gear
and mash her foot down
like her life itself might of depended on it
drove to town and come right here
where she was setting
when we heard the firealarm go off
and known something terrible had happened

even Sheriff Red Floyd sed
it was a tragedy to have such a thing occur
on a night when all the fireboys
was over to Tahoka playing softball
in the churchleague
wasn't nothing nobody could do
but let it burn

couldn't anybody on earth suspicion
she had one thing to do with it
I even myself calt Bryant Williamson
told him I'd take a oath to it on the telephone
she was setting right there
in that back booth where she comes
every night for supper

when that fire sprung out like a volcano
you can see the table right there for proof
he could make his choice for it
to be Henry Wheaton or a act of God
but it wasn't no way
she could of had one thing to do with it
I bet you boys done seen her in here
you can swear that's the truth
if it comes down to the need for it

I sez E.U.
in my pickup driving us out to work
you know more'n I do about all that
you believe in walking-round ghosts?
he say I don't know nothing
about nothing to say in no court
but I'll tell you
Henry Wheaton he aint no happy man
but I done got him settled in
saying more'n that bout that it won't be me
just like churchhouse or election
people believe what they gone believe
it aint no facts gone stand in their way
if they call it a ghost or a act of God
they won't go looking for some hired man
or kid or Ellis Britton or you or me
it'll be justfine left alone
let them go along their own way
I aint gone mess with none of it
or make myself not welcome in there
tomorrow yesterday or today
cause for us it's only one place
to get morning coffee and hear a good story or the news
and it's right there in Mr. B.L. Wayburn's cafe

Righteous

TOM CHRISTENSON

PARAGONAH – Tom Wayne Chris-
tenson, age 82, passed away on Nov
28, 1994, at his home in Paragonah.
He was born Nov 26, 1912, in Hick-
ory Flat, Miss., to A. Johnston and
Marjorie Mael Christensen. He
graduated from Searcy Jr High
School Ark, then moved near Para-
gonah where he farmed and lived
alone. Reverend Boyde M. Chiling-
ham stated that he was a very kind
person and was so loved by all who
knew him. He placed his faith in
church and the Lord.

Funeral services are Tuesday, Dec. 1
at the Paragonah Assembly for God
at 2. Burial will be at Terace Mound
Cemetery under the direction of
Huffman Mortuary Rufus Garner
officiating.

He sed the world
it wasn't no fit place
to live in for decent people
spent his life watching
it get worse and worse

ever year the Lard waited
to make itself known

and burn it all up with hellfore
till he got so old
he couldn't wait no more
so he died in bed alone

The Relic

*That since you would save none of me, I bury
some of you.*

JOHN DONNE, "The Funeral"

1

Ross Bearden celebrated
by going up to Montana
to be in the mountains
walk around by himself
alone with his vacation from work
for a week to clean out
except he took a wrong turn
doubled back past his starting place
sat facing the wrong direction
got up lost and wandering

in the forest
for over a month given up for dead
after they found his car
and put it on the radio and then TV
all the way back here
to find out who they could say
was the unfortunate lost soul
dead in the wilderness

man in a pickup found him
laying on the graveled road
thirty-eight days later not three miles
from where he'd left his car and tent
his whole body a scratch mark
or bruise you could hold
in a dishpan and run water on it
didn't look like he weighed

more'n a hundred pounds
half in and out of the ditch
tongue swollen up black
couldn't even say Hidy

at the hospital they knew
he was about to give it up
if they didn't get him dinner
so weak you could almost put your fingers
around his arms and legs
eyes sunk back in his head
like a John Deere 2-lunger
with the spark plugs took out
throat so dried up
no way he could swallow
found it unusual they sed
the number 30
he must have carved with a stick
on the inside of his arm
scratch lines all underneath

took them about eighteen tries
to hit a vein all fallen in
on top of each other
like a caved-in barn roof
to get him something from a bottle
when it started pouring
blood came out those scratch wounds
and bruises like a sieve
so dried up he couldn't
cry or spit or even bleed
sed they didn't know how
he could live through it
he showed them

2

sed he didn't remember
ever thinking about eating
after a week without
remembered falling in water
recalling what it was to drink
and a vision of a brown bear
then a lion staring at him
went on along
wasn't enough left to be
worth the trouble to chew

remembered thinking
about taking his mother's name
like the Mexican people do
thought he'd get more confused
so he let names go too

lost count of the days
numbers ran together
until the only one
he wasn't even sure of
was the one he was in
laid under a tree and laughed
at a daytime white moon
tried to fool him
into thinking it was night
time for him to curl up
and go to sleep

3

B.L. Wayburn asked him
what it was kept him alive
all them days

after he should have been dead
we all even Coy Stribling
came over to hear the testimony

was it the will to live
or the fear of the Lord
or the desire to die at home in bed
or the need of friends
or plain bullheadedness
or it all wrapped up in a bunch
we all wanted to know
was it an act of love?
he sed It wasn't any of the above

sed once when it was
almost the worst
there was a day
he took out his billfold
before he threw it on the ground
remembered a piece of his wife's hair
and a picture he carried
by his driver's license
took it out and swallowed it whole
sed the thought of leaving it
there in the forest after he passed
knowing nobody would ever find
their way back to the site
was enough to want a second chance

sed the divorce wouldn't be final
for a month
that was why he came
to last at least that long
and be found alive

or that creature would get everything
instead of just half

the thought of that
and the thought of his wife's hair
working in his guts and then
spewed out across the Montana dust
he knew he could always remember
that vision of his life
that was all it took
and that was enough

The Legend of the Monster
in Two Draw

Place where we'd swim on posted land
we had to cross the Bird Ranch to get to
was called Two Draw back then
before those three boys saw that creature in the water
and the town had to build a swimming pool
for it finally to stop the Second Coming
and keep Kay Stokes from bankrupting the county
then they named it Stokes Monster Lagoon

the boys were fishing without permission
when it got hot on a day
so they could put their fishing poles
with a rock on them
went down to the other side by the deep end
where the tree limb hung over with the rope
like all the other towns have there
so they could go swimming
and practice hanging themselves
had all the clothes off ready to jump in
when it was a miracle
that tank water commenced to churning up
like spoilt beer foaming out the still boiler
all this moss came off the bottom fifteen foot
you could see crappie fishes running down
to the other end and they sed
they never knew it was so many
turtles in there everywhere getting out
these two black humps came up in the water
on top banging and sloshing but no yelling
at first about three foot across

after a week it was up to four or five with eyeballs
and arms down under the water they couldn't see
then just sunk back down
it might have got real quiet after that
nobody knows because those boys
didn't wait to find out
Billy Ray Bilberry got almost two miles
down the road before he remembered
his clothes hiding under a rock by the tree
he squatted in some bushes that didn't cover him up
while the other two ran on in to town
till he got so sunburned because he was redheaded
he looked like a duroc hog with water blisters
on its ast and freckles that went all the way down
years later when he's grown up
his wife sed They's all over him and stayed for good
because of what he seen in that tank

one of the otherns Bubba Bowen I think
had on only drawers and a tee shirt running
but called Billy Ray's house anyway
his daddy had to come get him with the car
he wouldn't go back he's so ascairt
none of those boys would for a week
somebody else stoled the clothes
and all the fishing poles they sed
one even had a catfish on
the boys didn't even care about no more
they couldn't have been more famous
if they'd been killed or went blind on bad whiskey
they broke in and stoled from a shiner
in one day everybody around known
by a week it got so bad they had to
call a town meeting so they could

keep all the people scared to death about it
for something to worry and call each other liars over
besides the churchhouse and town council
A.N. Lucas was mayor back then
but he couldn't even get them to shut up
so he could call it to order
Mizrez Fortune who was arredy eighty
sed it was dark shadows
crawling in the alleys she'd seen at night
probley out there to rape her in the dark
while she's looking at the neighbors' windows
with her binoculars all alone
without a husband she could really use now
two of the hired hands over to the No Lazy S
sed they'd swear to an oath
it was flying saucers mutilated
forty-two head of cattle across the nation
that the insurance had the responsibility to pay for
and cut all their privates off
Kay Stokes had wrote their testimony out
on a piece of paper for them to read
then Coy Stribling stood on a chair
with his blue Newtestament they give his kids
up to the junior highschool before they quit
and ran off in his hand reading out loud
about the Nicolaitanes which he hated
but we hadn't met yet so we had to wait awhile
he read how it was a bottomless pit with smoke
of the furnace by reason of the dark air
and scorpions having hair as the hair of wormen
and then a dragon casting out a flood from his mouth
with the arms of Gideon
which was a prophecy of the Lord which sez
he's gonna show unto us Jeremiah's whore

coming up out of the water
with one hand full of abomination
and the filthiness of her fornication
in the othern

well that got even the Baptists
because we knew that's what them boys
been talking about
they couldn't deny it
It was a sign from God Coy sed and read
the Second Coming was at hand
to wipe out all the dogs and whoremongers
and murderers and idolaters
and whosoever loveth and maketh a lie
right there in the book word for word
spewing hot and cold out the mouth of Jesust
he had us all going straight to hell
if we didn't get right to the churchhouse
with money for the collection plate
it was wormen bawling and men
promising to pay up debts
and stay out of the beer joints in the flats
all over in there
one of the three boys was about to have
an espiscoleptic fit he was so ascairt
from what he'd done that very day
he sworn out loud he'd cut the palm of his hand out
with a butcher knife or a meat axe
before he'd ever touch hisself with it again
he was sure he was the reason it happened
because the Lord had been watching
him do it in the garden
he known it'd be white hairs of the heathen
growing all over and out it by judgment day
he could feel hisself going blind

some of the Pennycostals were ready
to go to their churchhouse and get snakes
and jars of poison for testimony
sed all them people was so worked up
they's ready for it by then
and the fat womern could jump the benches
started clapping singing Jesust saves
until A.N. Lucas finally got Sheriff Floyd
to get Coy Stribling down off that chair
and that Newtestament in a drawer
so he'd shut up and they could have a meeting
and whoever else wouldn't close his mouth
would have to leave until he was called on
then sed What do we do?
Coy Stribling hollers Acts 2:38
R.B. McCravey sez That's it
I'm gone kill that sonofabitch
but Sheriff Floyd wouldn't let him
it was too many witnesses
they sed Coy could either leave right now
or not say another word until he had permission
R.B. moved over behind him
took out his pocketknife and started
cutting on his warts and fingernails
shaving the hair on his wrists and arms
Coy didn't say any more

Mayor sez We got the problem of a hysterical community
over a unexplained happening
we have to get to the bottom of
by using our common sense
so what DO we do now?
everbody in there had a rumor and an idea
some sed build a fence with barbwore

and electricity around that tank
Eugene Cummings sed A fence like that
never held hogs in even
if they'd get out whatall's in that water'd find a way to
come find us in the night
Mattie Lou Collier sed she was gone buy her
a shotgun and keep it in her closet
Mizrez Fortune sed Oh no
you got it all too crowded in there
it'd be better under the bed
where she could get to it
on the left-hand side by her blue houseshoes
Ellis Britton sed Throw dynamites in the tank
see if it'd come up and we'd line the banks
on both sides with rifles from the first amendment
shoot acrost the water
at each other to kill it
then it was a motion from Beulah K. Byrd
who was proud it happened on No Lazy S ground
to tear out the dam and drain the tank
so it wouldn't have no place to be
that we thought it was a pretty good idea
until Kay Stokes stood up and sed
Nosir gentlemen you are NOT
gone tear out no goddam dam on my property
while I'm alive I guarantee it for a fact
when the District Attorney Waymon Gamblin sez
It was in the interest and benefit
of the community Kay Stokes sed
Any one of you sets one foot on my ranch
by that tank I'll personally
have my Mexican hired hand shoot you
in the inarrest and benefit of the community
in the head or worst for trespassing

I'll take ever penny I own
out of the bank right on that day
this whole county will go under on the spot
because I own that bank
I'll buy a bankrupt sale
and bid on ever bit of it you think's yours
won't none of you ever get
one thing of it back so help me Joshera
Beulah K. Byrd can go straight to hell
if she thinks she's getting one drop of my water
you can write that down in the book
for judgment day

wasn't nobody sed nothing after that
Kay Stokes had that whole town by the short hairs
we knew he'd do it like he sed
wasn't nothing else to add up
then he sed If it's the Lard pissed off
like your Reverent Coy sez
well I don't blame him
it's time you stopped electing Republicans
and trespassing on private property
you keep your ast and your kids where it's posta be
none of this wouldn't happen
so if the Lard's got a problem
he can take it up with me
I done built a fence around that tank
now you quit crawling through it
stirring up things isn't none of your business
and none of this won't ever happen again
whatall's in that tank is on my land
if it aint human it belongs to me
if it is it probley does anyway
I don't want to hear nobody in here

even think about it again it's mine
so you get on home and watch television
that's all you dismissed
he set down and stared at us
until we figured out he was through talking
that was permission for us to leave
his courthouse so we did

it must have worked
nothing else happened
somebody put up a sign sed Monster Lagoon
by the fence that he kept
after he put Stokes on top
so they'd remember it was his
and spoiled the joke they'd made
a year later we didn't even think about it
that much any more except for kids
town finally passed a bond
to build a swimming pool
for something to do
of a summer when it was too hot
wouldn't nobody go out to Two Draw no more on a bet

it was four years later
my cousin by marriage to Tilda Sims
was working for No Lazy S Ranch
had to go down there to pull a cow
stuck in mud with a pickup out
worked half a day getting her loose
another two hours
keeping her from going right back in
had to herd her down to the one by the blue gate
on hardscrabble where she couldn't
find her a place to sink in to her armpits

getting a drink of water
sed while he's out there in that shinery
chasing that cow he about had a heart attack
run right up on this snapping turtle
looking like the biggest bloated baby elephant
he'd ever saw in his life
sed you couldn't of covered it up
with a number 12 warshtub
if it would of bit him
it'd take his whole leg off
just setting there by the tank
staring at him in the sunshine

Kay Stokes when he heard
calt him in sed
Son I'm gone give you fifteen dollars
to never tell nobody what you seen out there
that turtle is my property
and I'm buying the memory of it
right out of your mind
I own that too
I hear you ever told one person what you seen
you won't never work in this state again
even for Bryant Williamson
you better believe me good
you go buy your wife supper
at Wayburn's cafe on me tonight
and don't never remember nothing
bout this ever again
so that's what he did
for over a year
until him and my brother got personally drunk
one night and he told him in confidence
by swearing him to god he wouldn't never tell nobody else

but he told me the next day
pretty soon we all knew
but we also knew we couldn't tell
it was the official town secret
known only to Kay Stokes and by us

it didn't matter
we arredy had what we were going to believe
learned by heart
we had the swimming pool by then
the boys were famous
Coy Stribling took credit for stopping the Second Coming
with his testimony before the Lord
that doubled the collection plate at his churchhouse
for almost a month so he could trade his car in on a new
      used one
and we had a place to take the girlfriends
on a Friday night for wallering
where they'd have an excuse to be too ascairt
to get out and walk back to town in the dark
even at that age
just like religion and town council
that's there to hold the multitudes together
we knew it's some legends and opinions
you can't let facts get in the way of

Song E.U. Washburn Heard the Mockingbird Sing Near the Grave of Janie Grace Gosset

*Memory is a kind of homesickness – and like
homesickness, it falls short of the actualities on
almost every account.*

IVAN DOIG

Your life in the waking time,
my child, will find its glory
not in departure or fact
but inside the remembrance
and how that tale will be told;
life separate from its story
withers to bone, mute and cold.

Beneath a time, lovely one,
your life begins again here
where the longer we remain
the more those above recall
memories that never were.
Beyond time and waking sun
you may believe it as well.

Just as your tale, my sweet one,
cannot be removed from place,
shape forms as story is told.
This the glory that lingers:
each telling is new and whole,
blossoming into full song.
Each singing births a new soul.

Stranger

B.L. Wayburn one morning
was telling this new customer
who came by himself in a car
selling Perkins flowerseeds
Jim Heynen's story about the three boys
went in the filling station bathroom to pee
saw this money in the pisser
filt up with somebody else's business
so they was all kindly upset
had to figure out what comes next
if they flush it all that money go down
but they caint put their hand in that mess
to get it out so what would he do?

before he can tell him what's right
how they all put a nickel in
then pee on it to up the ante
and walk off for somebody else's problem
Ellis Britton he hadn't been paying attention to
being mad at the world by himself
at the end of the counter
jumps up and grabs
an empty waterpitcher
runs down swinging that thing
like a twelve-year-old boy chopping cotton
knocks that man's breakfast in his lap
breaks two cups of coffee
and a glass of ice water
gets right in that poor
flowerseed salesman's face
whose story it wasn't even

hollers What kind of a trashy
sonofabitch are you anyway?
I'd tear that goddam toirlet off the wall
burn that filling station to the ground
if you done such a thing in this town
don't you never come here
with a damnstupid idear like that
where it's decent people
you go on home wherever that is
and don't never come back here again

went right out the front door
without even paying for his coffee
got in his truck
with the waterpitcher in his hand
and went and drove off and left
without saying no more

that man had scrambled eggs and
bacon with ketchup and a bite of lightbread toast
in his mouth he couldn't even swallow
setting there with the rest of his plate
on his shirt without any napkin in his lap
wondering what he was posta say
what in the hell wrong did he do

B.L. Wayburn sez Well mister there you go
that just goes to show
when you telling a story next time
it's one thing you better do
you best look around and make sure
which kind of stranger or friend
you telling it to

Private Conversation Overheard from the Booths: Eulogy After the Fact, or Reflections on a Gift from a Magus

MATTHEW 25:40

It was a day in August
after the County Fair
this boy was walking a forty-pound shoat backward
he won in a greasepig chase
up a gravel road
with a bucket over its head
nine years old when Bryant Williamson
drove his pickup right there
rolled down the window
spit Brown Garrett snuff on the ground
sed What's that hog?
boy sez It's mine
he sed I can see that
it's the one with the bucket on its head
where you going to with it?
boy sed From that cedarpost yonder
by the powerpole four more miles

Bryant Williamson asked him
Hasn't nobody come along this way?
boy sed Just one truck
from No Lazy S
it never stopped just honked to get by
Bryant Williamson sed I don't mean to be polite
and speak ill of them I wish was dead
but them's Kay Stokes's hired hands

and he is one sorry sonofabitch
I'll testify that to a oath
boy sed I know it

Bryant Williamson sed Hogs are like Democrats
they won't lead and they won't foller
unless they real hungry
and you got a full bucket in your hand
you might as well put it
on their head and go backwards
boy sed I know it
Bryant Williamson sed You want a ride?
boy sed If you aint got no wheelbarrer
that sounds fine

him and that old man
wallered that hog by its tail and ears squalling
to be heard twelve miles like an insane man
whose wife lost his mama's handkerchief
into the back of his truck
tied its feet up with baliwore
so he could sit up front
and look out the window driving
four miles home

Bryant Williamson sed That's a fine Christmas pig
boy sed Nosir it aint
I'm having babies with it
he look back at that barrow
say I believe we may have another star
rising in the east by then
boy sez I know it
never sed no more
drove him and his pig home

unloaded them and got it in the pen
fixed a gate to hold it in

next part I have to make a guess at
but he must of drove
a hundred miles that night
to find a black listed forty-pound gilt pig
twin of that greased barrow
how he got her swapped in that pen
without waking up that boy
I didn't find out for ten years
until the day they had his funeral
R.B. McCravey told me
he bought a five-gallon bucket
of sour mash right out of his still
so he could get two pigs drunk enough
to load them without a squolt
sed if anybody ever ast one word about it
he'd see they got sued from both sides
and died with unpaid insurance
that was a fact

that boy had his pig more'n nine years
she farreled almost 200 head of babies
got him raised and through the FFA
eat up ever beet in the garden four times
and I believe that bucket's still around
hanging on a nail in the barnloft
if it's a need for it

they say it takes three turns
done for the doing and kept a secret
to get to heaven
Bryant Williamson was crooked and rotten
as a doughty aspen

Kay Stokes told that to everbody
who would listen to hear it
and he was too rich to argue about it with
but I know personal of two he had on account
as long as Kay Stokes aint the Good Lord yet
it's at least a small chance he might of made it

The Fish

… victory filled up…
from the pool of bilge
where oil had spread a rainbow…
… until everything
was rainbow, rainbow, rainbow!

ELIZABETH BISHOP, "The Fish"

Arty Gill went down
to the cafe that Saturday morning
to have coffee with the boys and that's all
until he found Cephas Bilberry and Roy Talbert
ready to go fishing and he knew
that's what he wanted to do too more than life
even bought an extra case of Lucky Lager
so they could make sure
they all had good times
he was as happy as a goose
that found him a half pound of raw bacon
his wife Modean had to call B.L. Wayburn
at 10:12 that morning waiting long enough
for him to get done and back home for chores
to find out where he was
didn't even come home to change his clothes
only thing she'd told him he had to do
that day was fix the shelves in the closet
and clean out the storage shed
so she could get to the canning jars
with maybe one or two other odd jobs needed doing
he was going to hear about it
when he got back for sure
B.L. Wayburn sed he expected that to be a fact

didn't get home till after dark
all three chasing beer with whiskey
thirty-two fish in two towsacks
a pound or better one catfish
upwards of six to eight they bet
poured them all in the kitchen sink
went to the living room
sat down on the furniture to tell each other
how it had been catching them fish
one more time till they all three
went to sleep sitting up in their chairs
except Arty laying on the long divan
Modean never even came out
of the bedroom to look at the fish

woke up about three in the morning
to pee bad all that beer moving
Roy Talbert in the bathroom
being sick with the door locked
Arty couldn't wait he went to the sink
there was all those fish
his wife hadn't even
cleaned up yet he sed
the smell of it almost turnt his stomach
made him so mad he's ready
to knock down that bedroom door
make her get up and do those fish right then
had to hold them apart with his hands
all sticky and smelly so he
could see to hit the drainhole
if he hadn't been so dizzy from the whiskey
he'd of brought it all to a end
right then he had to lay down
room was circling him bad

when he got up Sunday morning
bedroom door still shut
he could tell she'd come out
about had a brain spasm when he saw
that trashy womern had made her breakfast
piled the dirty dishes after eating
right on top of all them fish
laying goggle-eyed waiting to be cleaned

he had it he went right to that door
sed Modean you in there?
jiggled the knob to see it was locked up
sed You come out here right now
get this kitchen all cleaned up
you beginning to embarrass me
saw Cephas and Roy Talbert staring at him
waiting for her to come put coffee on
sed Come on out of there Modean
wasn't no sound from that door
smacked his hand on it flat sed
You get on out here right now
get these goddam fish and dishes out
of this dirty sink and in the frigerator
you listening to me?
still wasn't no sound sed
You testing my patience I'm warning you

she sed then from inside the room
I'm not touching them fish Arthur
you can do whatever you and them two men
sleeping in there with you drunk
want to with them they're yours
he sed You say what? hollering by then
sed You heard me

I'm not coming out there till
you got that kitchen all cleaned
like it was when you come home
forty-two minutes after eleven o'clock last night drunk
he said Modean it aint my job
cleaning no kitchen with your dishes
I never messed up you come out that door
she wasn't talking by then
went in set down staring back
at Cephas and Roy Talbert
neither one offering any advice for once
just wanted coffee like it was supposed to be
hollered finally They'll lay there
a week before I'll touch them
real low they heard her say Fine
he said Two weeks by god
real low again she said
You drinking up your prime water
made him mad as a wagon
to be talked to that way in front of his friends
whether they's drunk or not didn't matter
jumped up and run to that door
smacked it with his fist screeching
like a hog being nose-ringed
You open this goddam door right now
I'm gone bust it off its hinges
stepped back and lowered his shoulder
bunched up to butt it down

door might as well of been invisible
or made out of glass
they heard the bolt slide open
sound of a shotgun shell
pushed in the breech

then the bolt close
like it was right there
in front of all six eyes open not blinking
Arty on one foot getting ready
to rooster fight that door froze in ice
Cephas and Roy Talbert putrefied
on the front of their chairs
then like an icicle melting come back
set that foot down
turned his head back at them
sed I believe she's ascairt enough
maybe I better let off the pressure
they both sed they believed
he was exactly right
wasn't no use to even talk about it
they better get on home now it's late
went out the front door
without even dividing up the fish

sed he couldn't stand it in there no more
all that cold air and dead fish
put on his hat and went
to the cafe for his coffee
wouldn't even talk to nobody about it
because they hadn't found out yet
when he got home she was gone

pushed him one too far he sed
made him some breakfast and thrown
his dishes in there with hers
on top of them fish in the sink
then dinner and supper when she
wasn't back from running off yet
including bologna rinds and bread crusts

he put water on so they'd stay soggy
slept on the furniture by himself
so when she snuck in late she'd see
he wouldn't sleep in that bed
with or without her by god
it was a matter of principle

third morning he got up looked at that sink
flooding over with dishes and garbage and fish
got so mad he stood there and hollered
at her by name for ten minutes
then run to that sink started throwing
everything in it out on the floor
fish stiff and crooked
all but one he couldn't believe it
that big catfish on bottom still alive
buried under there waiting
its mouth going open and shut gasping
for clean air as much as he was
thrown it on the floor and watched it flop
walked out the door and went to the cafe
had to sit by himself at the counter
had the fish smell too bad in his clothes
even Tommy Minor had a hard time
walking by him didn't even
hide that it was a task worth wages
Arty walked a path around them fish
all the rest of the week stinking
had to open all the windows
to let air in and out

drove to Tahoka on Sunday
to see if she might be over there
let her apologize if she'd had enough

nobody had heard of her they sed
Monday he couldn't take it any more
went in to look at the fish
saw them flybloat and oily
thought he'd proved his point
it was almost a week and a half
studied for a hour in the door
called Huffman Furniture to see
if it was any way they could come out
lay a sheet of linoleum over the top
mash it all down in between
Victor sed he'd send Ardell down
next morning but when he come he sed no
wasn't no way that'd work
he'd have to get it all up first
Arty sed what would he take to do it?
Ardell sed he didn't need no money
that bad yet he'd have to pass

Arty called every housecleaner in town
starting off with Juanita Valdez that day
they all sed no they wouldn't
word got out most wouldn't even
talk to him on the phone sed
they wasn't home and wouldn't be
for a long time more like his wife sed
he was on his own

must of urped upward of a dozen times
during them latter days
where he wasn't lying any more
when he called in sick to work
they seemed to know it
come to the cafe they wouldn't ask

just bring him thin soup and coffee
at the end of the counter
with the door open for the air
even Roy Talbert didn't set with him
we wouldn't of thought he'd of noticed

Friday went with a grain shovel
and a sheetrocker's gas mask on his face
in that kitchen with the house opened
scraped up everything hadn't melted in
the floor and thrown it to his pickup
in a barrel so rotten it ruint it where
you couldn't even haul pigfeed
drove it out to the dump ground
where they made him pay four dollars
to unload in the dead-animal pit
couldn't even leave the barrel there
had to crawl back in and pour it out
haul it over to the landfill
so they could cover and bury it up

went home poured coal oil and turpentine
ammonia and Turtle Wax mixed with fly spray
on that floor until it looked like gravy
washed it out the door with a water hose
did it again twicet more
sed if it didn't get it out that last time
he was ready to burn it down
with or without no insurance
warshed up all the dishes he hadn't ruint
took all his smelly clothes
to Isaacson's laundromat and gave that girl
six dollars to run them through
as many times as it took

to get all the fish smell out with Clorox
went home and took a hot bath
with half a bottle of shampoo
four squirts of Wildroot hairoil and a bottle
of lemon juice with Babo stirred in the water
to get it out of his system

at the cafe they all sed
he looked to be a new man
let him have his coffee in the booths
with the people up front
he sed he couldn't eat yet and it might be
a long time before him and his appetite
could get back on speaking terms
he was just glad to be alive
he'd never again wonder how
it might be to live with Wesley Stevens
or be one of the Bullards

come home he couldn't believe
if it was a vision or the devil
Modean in the kitchen standing by the stove
cooking supper in fried grease on top
sed his knees went loose and he retched
out loud at the thought of fish frying
or being cooked in there in any fashion
she sed Warsh up if you gone eat supper
he couldn't take no more suspense
or tragedy in his life that day
held his breath and leant in to see
beans in a pot and fried potatoes
in a pan and a cut-up
chicken in that boiling grease
it was almost enough to make him

think he could ever be in love
with a womern like her again
changed his mind on the spot
didn't make her apologize
in public of her misbehavior and negligence

sed it wasn't worth it
it was all water under the boat in the past
he'd learnt a lesson to be learned
never again would he ever
bring home that many fish
to set in the sink more than one night
before he'd find a way
to get the neighbors to take some
even if he had to pay them to do it
and trying to find something like that
to get out of cleaning the storage shed
wasn't no way worth a new $200 kitchen floor
to save what's left of his
not very good in the first place marriage
sometimes it's best to not fish or cut bait
but just get the chores all the hell over with

Land:
Overheard Coffeecounter
Conversation between Charlie Parks
and Tommy Minor

For immediate sale: 300 acre parcel, largely
undeveloped rangeland. No water rights.
Call Bryant Williamson, Jr. Realty,
Williamson Associates. #426

I don't expect you to understand this, son,
but I swear to God
I did not purposely design that ranch
as a nonprofit institution.

A Hymn for Pearl

A day none of us who were there
will ever forget was when
they buried Pearl Nance
who wanted more than any woman
ever lived not to be one

from the time she was twelve
she was God's experiment in gravity
any part you would have thought
could stick out got too big
pointed straight down
even her neck was a broken swivel
where her head studied only sidewalk

wore men's britches and boots
snap-up-front shirts with W.B. Garrett brown
and fingernailfile snuffmop in the pockets
she could hork and spit and curse and lean
into a pickup fender
never did get the rhythm
to make it seem recreational
wasn't nobody to fault her
for not making the effort

it was a Thursday oncet
she went behind the cafe counter
late for evening coffee with this pint
she brought down from Johnston still
poured half a filled cup brimful
sed Here Brother Coy
let me buy you coffee this one time

him setting in his booth alone
like the cormorant in the tree
in the garden of life
with a harpoon to shove into any words
he heard and thought fit to drag up
for one of his sermons he brooded on
as a responsible affliction for the Lord
to visit on each and all of his many enemies
him and the Lord shared
in their enthusiasm for the gospel

only thing he could think of to say was
Why thank you ma'am
us struck as dumb as Zacharias
our meditation on the wish for his death
interrupted for the moment
and then: Why this here coffee has some bite to it
and then: Is it any possibility of a refill?
to which:

Pearl sed Let me bring you
a fresh cup Brother Coy
and then a third
and lo
him who we known as so filled with hate
he'd rot fast when he died
so E.U. always had a hole dug and ready for
ahead of time just in case
began to smile
began he to even laugh
for the first time we knew of ever

no one there could have predicted
the Lord's hand would reach out

and touch that one
it was a terrible mystery to us all
but when he stood and embraced Pearl
with a Christian's brotherly kiss
when she brought the fourth
it was a lesson
to never underestimate the power of the Lord
or the goodness of fine whiskey

and then she sed
Brother Coy I am become singful
and he sed Let us make a joyful noise
before the Lord
and began a spate of hymns
that tested the endurance of all the gods

fourteen times B.L. Wayburn had to unlock
the cafe door so half the town
and all the regulars could come in
until four in the morning from page one
"Trust and Obey" of Christian Hymnal #2
to "How Great Thou Art" pasted on the backside cover
memorized by heart in four-part harmony
plus two others unknown to music
so R.B. and Ollie could join
all together singing flatout

even old George Albany come in
the front door for oncet with his tray
and perfect-pitch tenor we never known of
did the solo in "Lead Shining Light"
Pearl rising to the occasion with her obligato
"Out of the Ivory Palace" Coy bawled on
and admitted for the first time

she thought in a previous life
maybe she'd been one of them eunuchs
in that Viennie boys' choir
and how much she must of loved it
as something to look forward to

Coy leading "I Come to the Garden Alone"
from the top of the counter
in between every stanza saying One more time
to tell the Lord you really mean it
so hot in that cafe by then
Baby Jesus was wilting off the inside cover
of the hymnals in their racks
in their pews in their respective churchhouses
scattered across the dark streets of our town
joined together for the first time in song
the only time any of us who knew him
professed any love for that sad man
and then she died

took three days to decide
she'd never been inside a churchhouse oncet
since she was old enough to choose
it wouldn't be right to inflict
the ceremony on her then
we all came to the graveyard instead

so many people they had to stand on chairs
and almost all the preachers including Coy
to see B.L. Wayburn speak the words
we all sed as testimony
over coffee he wrote down
how when he came to the part
She was the founder of the Thursday Night Choir

which only met that one time
it must have been the inspiration of the Lord
us all breaking out together at oncet
with "Just As I Am" flatout

every one of us there who known
could see with our eyes closed
her big chest swell up
knowing she wasn't no longer alone
till all those pearl snaps on her cowboy shirt
popped open one by one

A Tale of Ignorance, Stupidity, and Cold Beer without Moderation

Y'all hear what stupid damn thing
that Dickie Biggins boy done?
sed R.B. drinking coffee at the counter
we all sed No where? he sed
His daddy bought him a brand-new used car
that was a Chevrolet from Ed Power Ford house
so he got him some bootleg beer
went out driving on the backroads
must of been going fast
hit this turn he hadn't thought about
car hit that barrel-pit sideways
flipped it over about nine times
mashed in both sides and the top
busted every bottle of that beer inside
never even put a scratch
on that sorry Biggins kid or flung him
out the windshield that car
not even three hours off the lot

sed He crawled out the side window
set looking at the wreck like a cow
found him a new gate he hadn't seen before
over a hour waiting for somebody
to come find him to see if he was injured
have to call the ambulance for him
or see if they could get that car to start
then got ascairt he'd never be found
and die of thirst in the wilderness
out there too far for him to walk to town
on such a hot afternoon

not a single unbroke bottle surviving
only thing he could think of to do
was send up a signal to the distress
so he taken his cigarette lighter
out of his pocket and started that car on fire
smoke come up like the courthouse burning
sed he's afraid he might get injured
in the explosion when it got to the gas tank
so he run back across the other side
of the road and hid behind a mesquite tree
so he could see if it happened finally
to tell what it might of looked like
till Jerry Stone seen the smoke from his house
not two miles away and come to see
what was burning up
sed that boy about scared him to death
come up behind him and sed Hidy
he sed Jesus on a frog pond what you doing?
boy sed could he get a ride back to town
so he could call and tell his daddy
what happened before he found out
by the rumor while he was standing
studying that car burning up by the road
R.B. sed he believed that was about
the most ignorant thing he'd ever heard of
an almost grown-up man even thinking
of doing in his life

we couldn't be sure that was first place
for that boy even if we considered
remembering the skunk he killed
in the living room of his own house
but Ollie McDougald sed he never
heard of that before

so Shorty Hamilton sed Ohyas
it was when his folks left him alone
to go on a vacation for themselves
for a week without locking him in the jail
and too far to haul him to the insane asylum
for their own personal safekeeping
so they left him in the house to live
taking care of himself for only a few days
in the summer when it wasn't that hot yet
sed he couldn't make it comfortable enough
too cold with the air conditioner on
in the room with the TV
too hot with it off so he opened
the door and run it on high
for the balance then went to sleep
setting in his daddy's fold-back Barcalounger
drinking J.L. Biggins' Pearl coldbeer

this skunk must of smelled the air-conditioning
come while he's sleeping in that house
sed that boy thought he heard a burglar or
something in his dream
scratching round on the floor
woke up and saw that creature in there
where he wasn't posta be
couldn't think of nothing to do
but run into his daddy's bedroom and get
his bow and arrow in the dark
stuck that skunk like an English schoolteacher's screwing post
to the living room floor pissing
all over the walls and floor with a flashlight
in his mouth to see by to shoot
B.L. Wayburn sed that was the Lord's truth
boy slept outside after that

on his mattress he drug through the kitchen
out on the frontlawn with dirty sheets
and set on the backporch in the shade
among the used Pearl beer cans
waiting for them to come back home
and clean up the mess so he
could have his own room back for privacy
had to eat canned goods out of the pantry
stench so bad he wouldn't let him
come in the cafe to set down
or eat out back even
smell come through the window
so bad catfish or turkeys would gag on it

and that might of truly been stupider
had to tear up all the carpets
and throw out the furniture ruint
cost them upwards of four thousand dollars
to get away from that boy
for less than a week
not even considering the loss of Pearl beer
they had to haul it all off
Huffman Furniture hired hands wouldn't
come in that house till that skunk
and most of the smell was gone
Ollie McDougald sed he was amazed
he hadn't heard of it before
but that was damned ignorant for sure

O'Dean Bloodworth sed No
that wasn't ignorant that was stupid
Ollie sed it wasn't no difference to speak of
he sed Oh yes it was
ignorant was when that foreign tourist

from California run out of gas
out by the Hurricane Ridge three years ago
he wondered if that Biggins boy
might of been remembering
if he could even think back that far
didn't know where he was
so he stayed in his car seventy three years old
for two days and died of the heat frustration
with the windows rolled up and doors locked
so nobody could sneak up and rob him
not even two miles from paved road
in the summer when it was a 100 degrees
wrote it all out in his diary as a testimony
sed his last wish was for an icecold bottle of Pabst
when they found him flybloat and dead
on a Thursday waiting to be saved
we all sed that was true we heard it
but Ollie he might have a point
of the similarity between the two

O'Dean got his hair up sed
It's a ignorant man might for instance
believe in something like ghosts
but it's a stupid man would believe
Henry Wheaton's ghost might ever
waste the energy alive or dead
to burn down his house
it wouldn't be worth the effort
and anybody who could think one bit
could see that for a fact
between the two

B.L. Wayburn cut right in sed Gentlemen
I can prove to you for a wager

of my ten dollars to your one
maybe not necessarily the difference
but make it a satisfactory separation
and also certify for a fact
who is the stupidest living man
in this town at the same time
and also the single most ignorant one
if I don't you don't have to pay me
one thing for it
I'll admit I was wrong in front
of the postoffice while I kiss your butt
and give you thirty days to draw a crowd
and buy each one a coldbeer from my own pocket
we'll assume we all done shook on it
unless you decide to back out right now
anybody who drinks morning coffee at that counter
and it was a fact that
not one of us got up to go and leave

So it was this other boy he sed
over to Fluvanna you probley never heard of
but his daddy we'll say bought him
this other used car and some bootleg beer
he could go out driving around with
upwards of ninety miles an hour
when he run that thing into a trestlebridge
we couldn't remember being anywhere near there
smashed that car up like a Berkshire sow
with the noserot's face
slung that boy up into the roof
so hard it torn both his cheek and nose off
to where they had to identify him
by his teeth marks on the steering wheel
left his brainpan in the dent

found his bottom teeth and one eyeball
under the frontseat
sed he was tore open like a viscerated butcherhog
after the scalding to where
they had to scrape part of him
off the floorboards with a putty knife
when they found him a week later
brains and liver and blood all over that car
wasn't even a hired preacher
in a hundred miles they could pay
to offer a prayer for that boy

it wasn't a sound in that cafe
for about eleven seconds
until back in one of the booths
Coy Stribling slid out and jumped up
like you'd hit his wife's second child
in the face with a scrubbing board
his little blue Gideon Newtestament
he was scanning for inspiration
for his Sunday sermon on temperance
he'd decided that very morning to preach
fell off the table on the floor
yellow egg juice running on his chin
his eyes so close together from the terror
you couldn't of drawn a pencil line
between them with a ruler
vein in his forehead stood out palpitating
didn't even have a napkin in his lap
fork and knife still in his hands
ketchup down the front of his shirt
sed Did it kill him any?

when we all finally looked back
B.L. Wayburn was sighting down a fly
setting on the counter rubbing his hands together
like a Reverend during collection plate passing
right after cotton ginning
took that dish towel off his shoulder
grabbed the ends and spun it tight
then like he had it between crosshairs
on a telescope smacked that fly
shot up about eight foot in the air
from the concussion never even
flopped its wings when it hit the floor
on its back with its legs sticking straight up
Poor ignorant creature he sed
ought to lock its mama and daddy inside
and burn down the shithouse
where that baby was created
left to hatch and grow up
for being so completely stupid to not warn
that child to come in a respectable establishment
and attempt to disrupt the influence
of polite conversation on a morning like today
stupefying the very air with its predictable buzzing
is what I have to say
why creatures like that is allowed by the Lord
to bear children to grow up ignorant
and then inflict themselves upon the world
I'll never understand
can anybody explain that to me?

in about thirty seconds R.B. McCravey
stood up and took out his billfold
laid a dollar bill by his coffeecup
walked out the cafe door

without even looking at Coy or B.L. Wayburn
then every one of us
at the counter did the same thing
got in our cars and drove off
without even talking about it
in the parking lot

cook leaning through the window seen it
sed Coy finally sed Well they must of done heard
B.L. Wayburn sed I suppose so
Coy sed then Well did he?
B.L. Wayburn sed No soon's he sobered up
they given him a transplant
he told them he had a vision of the Lord
told him to go back and try again
and remember the only unforgivable sin
was to participate in any kind of moderation
sed he was back in the school by Tuesday
two weeks later practicing for study hall
and besides he heard they might of been Catholic
and untruly washed in the blood of the Lamb
Coy sed Oh well then
set down and finished eating his breakfast
it wasn't any of his concern no more

evening here come Ellis Britton in his pickup
E.U. Washburn riding with him
so Ellis could tell him all the way
graveyard to the cafe how converting
from quarts and gallons to kilometers
was a communist plot to ruin the nation
take away all our freedoms to choose
and possibly even the right to bear and shoot arms
walked in without ordering nothing

Ellis sed Here's mine
thrown a dollar bill on the counter
E.U. sed I haven't got no dollar
I can give you this now
put a quarter on the counter
sed You can add a nickel a cup
on my coffee I'll get it paid up in a month
Ellis sed This is beermoney I expect
and I expect it's fairly earned and fairly paid
that's what we'll all say about it now

B.L. Wayburn picked up that money
sed Whatever's fair is fair gentlemen
sed Oh that a man's reach
extends to the end of his grab
or what else is a coldbeer for?
and for all the money in this town
that doesn't yet belong to Kay Stokes
and any he has left over to share
I wouldn't ever for all the world's care
want to be ignernt to real people
or stupid without reason in public
for even a minute
or let a friend stay drunk alone
without joining him in coldbeer
or endure scripture on it by the hour
not even for a second be moderate
without just and righteous cause
not for a heartbeat
let it ever be told I was unfair

E.U. Washburn's Story: Uncle Abe

I have not wasted my life.
RICHARD SHELTON, "Desert Water"

GENESIS 17:7

1

Oncet when I was a boy
a walking man come
to town twicet every year
folks didn't know who he was
name him Uncle Abe
sed he was lost and wandering
in his own mind
a harmless old thing just passing by

carried this paper bag in his hand
no child or cat can not find out what's in
I sidled him in the gravel road sez
Mister Man, what you got in that paper sack?

he turnt round looked me up and down
like a rooster hypnotized
by a line in the sand
sed Master Boy, I'll tell you what I brought
but you answer me first one thing
you say how many years your mama's got
I told and he sed not enuf
Tell me your grandmama's home
I sed she aint she's dead and gone

2

he say

    I was a almost whole live grown-up boy oncet
    like you walking along soon
    had me a paper sack of storebought candy
    going down the road
    after work at the cotton gin
    girlchild womern on her poach call me say
    Mister Man, what you got in that possible sack?
    come here show me right now
    patted beside her where for me to set
    I come to her she say What you bring?
    I shook all over
    she was beautiful as churchhouse sin
    I felt as ugly as the real thing

    she eat a piece without asking
    I known deep in my paper sack it was
    one chocolate covenant hiding to be last
    pretty soon we almost racing
    eating that candy so fast
    she lay one smiling piece on her tongue
    with her finger say come here
    put her mouth on mine
    she pass me that seed
    take it back again
    till the covenant was gone
    then so was she
    all but the memory

    I had me one wife, son,
    four good chirren grown up
    left and gone
    but never nothing

like that day since come along
now I got *hope* and *mebbe*
and then whatall time's left
this paper bag of sweet candy with one covenant
for her somewhere waiting
if I'm so blessed

3

he told me his story that day
again every time since twice a year
till the day he didn't come here
I never stopped remembering
the promise I made
to never have to say
I got no more of my life to waste
I still try to look
down every street
at every porch
every old walking man's face
every shadowed place

4

oncet Mama say
You don't be shiftless boy
don't you daydream your life away
pretty soon you be walking lonesome
empty head and pocket
like that crazy Uncle Aberham
kicking rocks down the gravel road
I sed Oh Mama Mama
don't even promise that might be so
it's a whole live world
inside that lucky man
you and all the rest of this town

don't even know
one sweet covenant
you can't never understand

Housedogs

Not louder shrieks to pitying heaven are cast,
When husbands, or when lapdogs breathe
their last

POPE, "The Rape of the Lock"

Ollie McDougald when I sat down
at the counter to have coffee sed
he didn't want to talk about it
I saw he's down in the mouth sez Whar?
he sed It aint nothing to speak of
I let it go and watched
while he stirred his coffee without any sugar
or milk in it with his spoon studying
sed finally If it's any of your buiness
it's that goddam fycet
my brother-in-law by marriage taken
and given to my wife she name Sweetie
now that sonofabitch lives in the house
all day and at night in our bed
it's about ruirnt my whole life
marriage done shot to hell
and dogshit all over the yard
what am I posta do?
B.L. Wayburn running coffee and cash register
listening in sez It aint nothing
about all this I don't know
so you curious you just axe me

I been married three times and had nine dogs
two of them in the house by two wormen
I'll tell you now free of charge

two things you can set your watch to
and live a life by if you want
first is a married womern can only love a thing
if she can pity it and run over it
which is why they let them things
set in their laps smelling them
watching TV in the house
whenever they scratch on the door to get in
and the second is what your daddy
should of told you in highschool that
a womern's love is like morningdew
sparkles like a diamond in a goat's ast
it might land on a red garden rose or a turd
it won't known the difference
you better make yourself accustom
she ever has to choose between you
and that shiteater you just as well
get on down the gravelway kicking roadapples
one of them might be dew wet
remember it caint necessarily help it
her and it just likes the shine
so all you can do is scrape off your shoes
come on in and set down
try to outlive it and not get anothern
that dog's as permanent and official
as Judge Parker in his courthouse
you want to stay married
make you a compromise and do it her way
that's all they are to it

Classified

I do professional quality FLORAL DESIGN if you will provide the materials and flowers. $6.00 to $12.00 per arrangement depending upon size. I am also selling some ORIGINAL POETRY which I wrote. Rights included. And; I do professional quality and HONEST HOUSE CLEANING. $7.00 per hour. No more than four to six hours per day at this time. No windows. I also do fine detail NEEDLEWORK pieces. No silk. Finished. In layed. or unfinished. Can be used in a variety of lovely ways. Prices vary according to size and detail. You provide fabric or buy my samples when available. You can contact me reguarding any of the above between 9:30 A.M. and NOON; WEDNESDAY THROUGH SATURDAY at 68 NORTH 800th WEST STREET (the same street as North 8th West) REAR SINGLE SOUTHWEST APT. #S.E. (second of two doors. First is #A. Second and last is mine – #S.E.) Paragonah 84740. I have no go-betweens and no phone or message phone. ALSO, KITTENS (not for fund raising, experiments or bait) need homes. HUMANE TREATMENT a must. See only myself, MAVIS TITTLE, about all these matters.

Conversation Overheard from a
Back Booth on a Tuesday Afternoon
After a Weekend Storm

1

"That man sitting beside you
last night at the party
what a nice man he was."
"Oh, Mama. Mama that man
he loves me. I think a lot."
"Yes baby girl. Surely
I did know that."

2

When I was a girlchild
oncet and I was
when Daddy worked in the mine
he brought all his possibles
and responsibilities home on the porch
for us not to touch on a weekend
that the Lord made for pure pleasure

it was on a Friday passing
into Saturday morning
after him being away all week a miner
making dreamplay in their room
all that house breathing love
and a whole live grown-up man
walking in a part of my mind
I didn't think my mama
knew about either
in the night

I had to go out on the porch
alone with him in the midnight
with a giant storm throbbing
all around and inside
so I had to sit down
on Daddy's box from the mine
I didn't find out until tomorrow
was dynamites for the blasting

it was a wonderful
terrible storm that summer night
whole sky and house filled
with fire and thunder from all the gods
my body drenched with rain and sweat
until my nightgown held on to me
like love itself

I sat alone
with the shadows after the storm walked on
breathing in all the rainwallowed hay
and the yard and Mama's roses
opened and shed across the garden
glistening in the dreamlight
the whole live world exploded
and brought back together
by what happened
to us all, baby girl,
in the storm that night

The Twenty-One Gun Salute

The next to the biggest event of the season
the year the Wheaton place burned down
was Leland Haygood's funeral
he'd been putting off two years
getting his hating arrears caught up
all put in order
finally got to it on a Thursday
when the wind blew all morning
went to sleep in his chair
woke up dead that afternoon

George Ann wouldn't have it
any other way but to send him off
like he was expensive
in the biggest casket we'd ever seen
wide enough to hold two of Leland
deep enough to throw in eight
of Bus Pennel's hounds and four raccoons
to chase bawling through immortality
with a water trough deep enough
to hold a four-pound catfish at the footend
eight pallbearers all sed made them
go to Bob Collier drugstore to find
a rupture truss and a tube of chapstick
to carry in their pocket for private emergencies
till their hemorrhoids sucked back in
so they wouldn't dry up and bleed

eight kind of prayers to grease the passage
singing to wake all three
of the triurnal host from their slumber
and rouse the everlasting eternities

down to the subaltern deities
and a plague and endurance of scripture
eulogy and sermon to put them all
back into the sleep of the angelic heavens
where even Mizrez Bouchier sed
she could feel her blood sugar dropping

Leland was a veteran and George Ann
wouldn't have none other than
a twenty-one gun salute and bugle music
at the graveyard with flag ceremony so B.L. Wayburn
got seven oldfart veterans of the big war
with Leland against the Kaiser
practiced marching in line
right-shouldering arms to be ready
went to Tahoka and borrowed
eight matching khaki shirts and brown ties
tucked in between the second and third buttons
VFW cocksucker hats for them all
so they'd look official before the Lord
but couldn't get them to borrow him
any military M-1 Garand rifles
to him for the occasion
had to go to Bill Edwards hardware
where all he had matching was five
12-gauge Mossberg pump shotguns
and two breech-break 10-gaugers
the kind we called thunder-rakers back then
that would have to be the best
they could do given the short notice
he didn't figure anybody would care
Leland was known to have poached
a duck or two off No Lazy S tankwater
he was sure he'd think it just fine

had that casket out of the hearse
and grunted over to the canopy in the graveyard
pallbearers squatted in the shade
so their testicles would drop back down
that hole big enough to bury an elephant
and on the slings for lowering
a song and three prayers and
a short sermon on the love of the Lord
for the prodigal son and the churchhouse
waiting to gather in the everlasting
to the arms of eternity
the multitudes ready for the benediction
B.L. Wayburn sed *A-ten-shun* loud
because Bill Edwards gave all six who wanted
earplugs for those shotguns except Leonard Askins
who was so deaf he wore hearing aids
in both ears hooked up to a electric megaphone
on his chest and still sed Huh
every third sentence till you'd have
to start over and tell it twicet
second time so he could lipread
turned up loud as it would go till he could hear
B.L. Wayburn call cadence and
give out orders to raise and shoot

Forward March! he hollered
them surviving soldiers of fortune paraded
in front of the canopy out to *Platoon Right*
and then *Squad Halt* one-two
Left Face! turned away so nobody
might get his head blown off if one of them slipped
holding their shotguns like rifles
in a seven-man line of their
as much as they could remember military best

hollered *Prepare to Fire!* all seven guns
come up like they were welded together
on a length of windmill sucker rod
those two 8-gaugers in the middle
with Leonard Askins in between
so he could see what to do
pointing at the angels out of the firmament
Ready! Aim! Fire! K-BA-BOOM
seven shotguns went off in a squatch
all of us proud knowing
they hadn't practiced with real guns before
percussion rolled back and made
the canopy flown up like a geyser shot off
under a fatwomern's skirt outside the grocery store
same time B.L. Wayburn sed *Ready!*
they all pumped and broke the breech
to shove in the next shotgun shell
for the second blasting Leonard Askins
sed out loud Holy Shit! from the line
tried to hold up his shotgun with one arm
turn down that transformer on his chest
with the other hand too late
Aim! he sed *Fire!* K-BA-BA-BLOOM BOOM
ragged this time like their sparkplug lines got crossed
and the muffler backfired Goddam
Leonard Askins yelled and tore
both them earplugs off his head
sound squalling through that hearing-aid box
like creatures was in there maybe
a duck and a weinerpig fighting it out
over a half-used ear of boiled corn
and the winner of it got to stay alive
dangling like Indian braids or two footlong
ear bobs down on his chest

Ready! yelled I caint hear while they pumped
and breeched and broke and loaded *Aim*!
I can't hear *Fire*! KA-BLA-BOOM-BOOM a goddam
BOOM thing! held his shotgun
above his head with one hand and pulled
the kick knocked that gun barrel
almost back into Ollie McDougald's face
he said Look out look out you sonofabitch
pay attention to what you're doing
Leonard hollering nine times as loud
as a pig stuck in loose wire like he was talking
to a Frenchman or Mexican who couldn't speak
any language trying to make him understand
I caint hear a goddam thing!

B.L. Wayburn yelled *Right Shoulder Arms*
Ollie did and jerked his head for Leonard
to straighten up and act respectable
at the funeral and get his gun up
hollering I think I been crippled by god
but he did too and turned back where they
came from except Leonard who walked
wouldn't even turn his corners
like a veteran of the lost wars slouching
boy from the highschool playing bugle
over the ceremony while they folded the flag
when he got by the people on the plastic grass
in the shade by the casket waiting
to be put down in the hole hollered
I think my eardrums done lasterated and broke
sounds like bombs went off in my head
I caint hear nothing!
like they all came there only to see him
standing all proper at attention

before the waft of bugle music
Ollie McDougald punched him in the butt
with his marching hand to keep him
moving on and from disrupting the services
so they could end the song
have one more endurance of benediction
let the Lord bend his ears
and receive his departed spirit
into heaven alone with the Baptists
go home and change clothes

then the line we all had to walk down
with the mourners and help make all survivors
terrible one last time in their grief
meet the Reverend Strayhan and Rufus
George Ann telling the veterans one by one
how proud Leland would have been
taken each of them up their fingers
shaken all their hands with tears
and sighs until Leonard come last
them earplugs still dangling
microphone on his chest turned up
where standing behind you could
hear every sound oncet and then again
a half second later like gospel singing
at the Campbellite church without a piano
to keep the music in a bunch
coming out those earpieces
sed Leonard I want to express my
he hollered My eardrums is bursted
I caint hear a goddam thing

Rufus leaned over and grabbed his arm
pulled him down the line
past the Reverend writhing in personal injury

over the sound of such a licentiousness
at this solemn and memorial occasion before his Lord
Leonard hollered at Rufus one more time
My eardrums done busted for life
tore through all the way into my brains
I never even liked the sonofabitch that much
Rufus leaned in to him and sed something
Leonard yelled Okay I'll wait over there then
went to the hearse and got in and sat down
acted polite to wait and have it done
didn't tell nobody else
he couldn't hear a goddamed thing

week later when we asked him
what he sed to have such
a wonderful calming effect
before the widow and the Lord's servant
he told us we all knew Leonard
could read some lips being deaf
known it had to come to the point
he whispered the one word that had to be what it took
and it was Coldbeer

and the line moved on
with the day and so did we
Rufus and E.U. lowered the straps
put Leland Haygood in the ground
rolled up the plastic grass and covered him up
took down the tent and it was done
then Rufus got in the hearse
to go to town and get his debt to Leonard paid
it was all over one more time
started up that big black car
him and Leonard Askins without saying a word
they both took and drove away

Slow

While his boy was off
being in the army B.L. Wayburn
hired Tommy Minor to work at the cafe
after they told him he didn't
have to go to school no more
wasn't worth the effort for anybody
sed he was a slow child
one of them borned of too elderly parents
the churchhouse spoke of
being especially loved by the Lord
because it wouldn't never learn to read
we supposed that was a fact
that boy was so innocent
he couldn't of found how to sin
if you took him to Tahoka
to show him where it was at

B.L. sed he only had one speed
that was granny
he wasn't nothing but careful
at everything he did
sed he never so much as broke
one glass or plate washing or stacking dishes
he could scrub on a counter for a hour
getting it all clean perfect
walk away from it
like he never seen it before shining
B.L. told the other hired hands
Don't never try to get him in a hurry
don't matter how busy the work got
he could only do it his way
that would have to be enough

mornings after coffee rush
he'd do counters
filling sugar then salt and pepper
without oncet getting them switched
bring coffee to whatall's still there
filling cups right to the top rim
where you had to lean and slurp
before you could pick it up
then go to the booths with forks and knives
napkins to get folded and neatened
most treated him special
left nickels and dimes for him to pick up
otherns would leave or go to booths
and have that smash-nose daughter
bring theirs to them
some acted embarrassed of Tommy
like they didn't know
he was in the same room
some just ignorant
some cruel

about the worst was Kenneth Bullard
call him down from the other end
every time he'd walk past on the counter
to bring him some Fresh hot coffee
not none with no film on it
hold on to his cup while he's trying
careful to pourn studying so hard
he's chewing his tongue
Kenneth move the cup a little
to make him spill holler
Watch out goddam you about to scalt me
lean back and laugh proud
like a Campbellite preacher

telling churchhouse jokes over for supper
when he got up he'd lay a penny
by his coffeecup say out loud
Here's a little something
for your college fund
up to Texas Tech Tommy
youg'n keep the change
for everybody to hear
never did notice nobody
trying to pay attention
he'd been a Bullard so long
he's used to being ignored

it was on a Saturday
of a month that hadn't been worth remembering
afternoon nobody in the cafe
Tommy rolled up his aporn to his waist
when it was his turn
walked out and went
to First National J.R. Potts Bank
to bring in his paycheck
and coffeecounter money
B.L. Wayburn showed him how to put
in a paper roll when it was enough for one
all in his bank account
how could it of been but Kenneth Bullard
in that bank right then?
leaning against the front wall
scratching on his privates and butt
when Tommy Minor come in with his wages
we all later thought was another act of God
started right in loud sed
Well lookie here what they let out
of the loony bin to come round real people

what you got there Tommy
in your hand that way
that your dishwarshing money
from down to the cafe?
har harred louder when Tommy turned round
looked at him standing by the wall
walked up to him like he was a new duck
swimming in the horse trough

probably should of let it go
but it was an audience watching sed
Let's all see your college education money
how many pennies is it makes a whole roll?
never saw his hand wad up tight
like a iron wrecking ball at the end
of a steel chain looping back
in a realchurch tower clock pendulum
till it got every link
stretched tighter than a top strand
on a frozen barbwore fence
sed I'll bet you got about enough there
to buy you a spelling lesson
or about four minutes in a algebrar class
down to the junior college your choicet
mebbe shown you different
between eggs and gravy
so you'll known which side of the plate
to lick before you warsh it
thrown back his head to hee har
those of us watching saw it
like a gonger on a ten-ton bell
remembering no hands over ears
too late uh oh uhoh
that fist come up from the bottom

of a waterwell on the caprock
every bit of Tommy Minor's body part of it
his toes hooked to the floor like
railroad spikes up his legs and butt
uncoiling like a steel spring
broke loose from a runaway flatcar
through his back and shoulder
that rolled-up hand rose like a fat moon
over Quitaque Peaks on a July night
so hot there was nothing to do
but stand and watch it climb the air

it was a double bang
pop thunk same time
like the echo of an echo
a volcano shooting off
couldn't have splattered more than that money
busting out both sides of his hand
Kenneth Bullard's head back on that wall
so hard it was a dent you could
hang a cantalope in and it would have stuck
all his legs turned putty
like Tommy Minor jerked his skeleton
right out through his mouth
he went down in a bunch
wadded up where he could have sucked his toes
eyes crossed almost into the same hole
then rolled back where he could watch
hair growing out the back of his head

Nickels Tommy sed forty in a roll F-O-U-R-T-Y
looked down at them left in his hand
turned then turned back and scattered the rest
like he was sprinkling sugar

or flower blossoms on him sed
slow over that thick tongue
You can keep the change
paper money roll floated down
on Kenneth Bullard
like a butterfly come to rest
openwinged on the top of his head

Irby Metcalf heard the sound
in his office telling Wesley Stevens
why it wasn't his fault
he had to turn down that loan
to buy 600 head of feeder hogs
and he would go to jail
if he burnt down his house that night
come out to see if he could surrender in peace
if it was a bank robbery in progress
Tommy Minor walked right by him
holding his hand where it hurt
looked up at him sed Been practicing
went out the front door and left

they didn't know if Kenneth Bullard
was dead and all his jawbones busted
but the Lord wasn't studying justice he lived
with nothing outside broke jawsockets
looked like Doc Kitchens
took out wisdom teeth
with horseshoe clippers and pliers
Tommy's hand swolt up
like a puffing adder's head
and Kenneth Bullard got his attitude alignment
adjusted a notch to the left
he left Tommy all alone from then on

after that but Tommy pretended
he wouldn't ever notice
J.R. Potts left that dent spot
in the wall at the bank
for many a many year
as a reminder to act respectable
in such a high-class establishment

B.L. Wayburn found all about it
at the Post Office talking at the window
to Phil Bouchier about the widow Wheaton
went to find Tommy Minor
see if he done lost his paycheck on the way
did he need him to make out anothern
and could he still wash dishes for supper?
found him sitting in the back booth
with a friend at the cafe
paycheck still in his shirt pocket
E.U. teaching him the words slow
and the hand signs how not
to keep it under a bushel
Lord he had to let his little light shine

Song E.U. Washburn Heard While Tending Roses over the Grave of Philemon and Baucis Rojas

1 CORINTHIANS 13:13

Amor, ch'a nullo amato amar perdona,
mi prese del costui piacer sì forte,
che, come vedi, ancor non m'abbandona.

DANTE, *Inferno,* V, 103–105

Is it true that Love is God? she asked.
And he said Yes, oh yes, it is true, my love,
but you must remember
to try and never believe it that way.

And then do you believe? she asked.
And he said Yes, I believe beyond death
in believing, yes.
That faith one can never fully give up,
there will always be doubt.

You must also remember to hope
and that in our language to wait
and to hope are one.
Espera, querida, espera.

And then what should I hope for? she asked.
And he said With all your heart
you must hope
that Love will keep believing in you.
Have faith in that alone

for only then will the world
as we believe in it continue
and that is God
and that is enough.

Old

GENESIS 32:24–30

And, hast thou slain the Jabberwock?
LEWIS CARROLL

Drinking coffee sitting in the booth
B.L. Wayburn brought the pot by sed
Y'all hear old Jacob Hamilton
got in a fight last night
beat himself up so bad
they had to call an ambulance
take him to the hospital?
No what? we sed
was it his wife again?

No sed B.L. Wayburn
I believe we got her took care of
I think it was the Republicans and missionaries
and his chainsaw way I heard it

we remembered him sitting
at the counter that day by himself
started arguing with his wife
been dead seven years more or less
sed I know all about you Dutch-Irish
you sonsofbitches fart all the time
whole cafe listening by then
yes you, Leah, do I seen you
fart at the suppertable
oh yes I did
I seen you Dutch-Irish sonsofbitches
hold on to the table and fart

you did it so you could get everybody upset stomach
and get all the dessert
but it didn't work did it?
I seen you come in a cafe
to eat there and fart in front of everbody
swinging his coffeecup round
in one hand and his spoon in the othern
till B.L. Wayburn come over sed
I believe you got her told Jacob
looked up like he never saw him before
coffee sloshed down his arm
all over the counter
till the look in his eyes started back sed
Set in the bathtub blowing bubbles
all over her
B.L. Wayburn sed But she won't now
you done got her told good
sat for a long time coming back
sed You goddam right finally
got up and went out to go
up Sawmill Road and cut wood

everybody ascairt someday
he'd start a fight with himself
and cut his leg off with his chainsaw
come up on him out there
he's always arguing about something
working alone without even a dog
to kick or throw rocks at

Bobby Tippits sed he got started
on himself at the bar after
only one can of beer
he knew it might be a long night

first time he checked
it was the damn missionaries
come knock on his door
so they could kindly let him know
he was all doomed to hell
left him books and papers to read with directions
where to send the check to be saved
then the forest service and BLM
changing wood permits last time
if you took out
that sonofabitch Newton Salamander it wasn't
no different between the damn Democrats
and Republicans anyway
they all just inarrested in getting reelected
all sorry goddamed excuses for human beings
if anybody thought to ask him about it
after only one beer

sed he went to pee
stayed in there awhile
Bobby got worried
afraid he might get so mad
he'd tear his pecker off and mutilate himself
all over the bathroom
went to see sed he's in his own face
in the bathroom mirror
over whether it's best to choke and
then pull the starter rope or pull first
then choke it off
Bobby sez he sed Jacob I seen you
do it both ways one time
they might work either way
sed he turnt round
sed That's right it don't matter which

get the damn carburetor clean
you don't have to worry about it
that's ezactly right

took him back to the bar
sed You okay? he sed Yas
he'd be going on home soon
turned down to help other customers
sed it wasn't three minutes later
he looked back seen old Jacob
spitting at himself in the barroom mirror
then he got horse-eyed
stretched up and swung on his reflection
spun him around on that stool
fell off down under the footrail
sed he was fighting and kneeing
had his head under the brass pipe
where he could of broke his neck
bellowing like a flock of roosters
sed he was so pissed off if he could of
got his head loose he'd of bit himself
had to get down on top of him
and hold him to make him stop
and come back from wherever he was
so far off inside his head
his feet never would catch up with him
all wide eyed sed Sonofabitch
married his own schoolteacher
divorced her when she got the cancer
Bobby sed That's right he's pure trash
hollered By god he could of
waited it out till she'd done gone natural
like the rest of us do
sed he could feel him start to relax
muscles up like steel pipes

for such a old man
sed I believe you took care of him good
Jacob Hamilton sed Sonofabitch
done broke my arm in two
looked and saw it over the rail
almost folded up in half

called the ambulance
Russell Waltrip and his boy Isarel come
put that arm on a board and got him up
sed they had to take him to the hospital
looked at that boy sed
Who you vote for? boy sed
I aint old enough yet
he sed Stay that way then
getting old's too goddam much trouble
looked at his daddy
Russell sed I split the ballot half and half
Jacob sez they all going to hell
don't matter which

I aint going in Heaven's gates
if they put them up there
you turning on the siren?
Russell sed If that's what you want
sed You goddam right
let them put him in the back
sed the last thing they heard him say
shutting the doors was
One of you Republicans has to break wind
I appreciate the window rolled down
let in some fresh air
start this sonofabitch up
let's see how she'll go

sitting in the booth with our coffee
at the Wayburne Pig
we could all hear those last words
with our eyes closed see that sight
then the crazywomern banshee
scream of the ambulance
and the flashing red lights
they took old Jacob Hamilton
away into the night

Epilogue Scribbled on Four Napkins and One Line on the Palm of a Hand While Sitting in a Back Booth with E.U. Washburn

1

B.L. Wayburn loved to say
After all's sed and done
around here more gets sed than done,
and I've come to believe that's best

It's all gone fast
the season, the year, our lives
in a whirlwind with fire and rain from the gods
tearing up the gift of good earth
and the faster it went
the more we could see the only thing
that changed was us and the calendar
All the rest stayed pretty much the same

2

Reverend Strayhan's fat wife
got fungus in her navel
that turned rot before they could
find it and get down to it
she died from the outside in
Coy choked on a dayold jelly donut
for half off with free coffee so bad
he had a double hernia

prayer and the Lord couldn't heal
so he wore a jockey strap and a truss
until Dr. Tubbs gave him the indigent rate
to sew his rupture shut
after he agreed we shouldn't have to
listen about the injustice any more

J.L. Biggins died of the heart attack
and Arlis Jamerson had such a stroke
he can only sit in a wheelchair and drool
but B.L. Wayburn's boy got discharged
for the convenience of the army
in time to come back and take over
the cafe after B.L. and the widow Wheaton
cashed in on the farmhouse fire and sold
the front half of the place to Sonny Gosset
who drilled a well and planted alfalfa
and gave a ninety-nine-year lease on the back 160
to Williamson's Associates on speculation
for a subdivision and trailerhouse park
after the insurance money cleared
so they could get married and go
on a honeymoon to Paris, Idaho
to see his kinsfolk there
and if it was time enough left
pull that little camper trailerhouse all the way
down to Carlsbad Caverns, New Mexico
so he could see for himself
what it was like to have his whole body
down in a hole besides a coalmine
where he could be like Moses Pharaoh
and reach out and feel the dark as black
as the inside of the Bible

3

E.U. sed oncet
that he heard the voices
while he was mowing
out to Mr. Cummings' place sed
The slipperiest thing on earth is time
what's coming sneaks up slow and quiet
like glue drying or road tar melting
but the past slides out the back door
like wishes and prayers covered with White Rose Salve
and chased by banshees

4

We got our gospel at the shrine
of the Wayburne Pig
where I learned to love the good news
from those old men more than life

E.U. and I had one unspoken wish
to someday sit in a front booth
and let our words mingle with theirs
until one Christmas morning in the mirror

there were faces we almost didn't recognize
behind Tommy Minor at the coffeecounter
and in a stroke blinding as Paul's Damascus light
we saw the evidence of the miracle of time

We had become a part of what it is
that we wanted most to say and do
and while that may not be churchhouse heaven
for the likes of me and E.U.

for the time being
it'll more'n do

5

That's all they are to it.

About the Author

Since the publication of his first book of poems, *The Porcine Legacy* (1974), David Lee has written a poetry unlike any in American letters. His poems are informed by a background that is unique to the world of poetry: he has studied in the seminary for the ministry, was a boxer and is a decorated Army veteran, played semiprofessional baseball as the only white player to ever play for the Negro League Post Texas Blue Stars and was a knuckleball pitcher for the South Plains Texas League Hubbers; he has raised hogs, worked for years as a laborer in a cotton mill, earned a Ph.D. with a specialty in the poetry of John Milton, and is now the Chairman of the Department of Language and Literature at Southern Utah University.

He has published ten previous books of poetry, and is publishing a companion to this collection, *A Legacy of Shadows: Selected Poems*. David Lee was named Utah's first Poet Laureate, has been honored with grants from the National Endowment for the Arts and the National Endowment for the Humanities, and has received both the Mountains & Plains Booksellers Award in Poetry and the Western States Book Award in Poetry. The recipient of the Utah Governor's Award for lifetime achievement in the arts, he has also been honored as one of Utah's top twelve writers of all time by the Utah Endowment for the Humanities.

Born in Matador, Texas, he currently lives in St. George and Pine Valley, Utah, with his wife Jan and children Jon and JoDee.

The Chinese character for poetry (*shih*) combines "word" and "temple." It also serves as raison d'être for Copper Canyon Press.

Founded in 1972, Copper Canyon publishes extra-ordinary work – from Nobel laureates to emerging poets – and strives to maintain the highest standards of design, manufacture, marketing, and distribution. Our commitment is nurtured and sustained by the community of readers, writers, booksellers, librarians, teachers, students – everyone who shares the conviction that poetry clarifies and deepens social and spiritual awareness.

Great books depend on great presses. Publication of great poetry is especially dependent on the informed appreciation and generous patronage of readers. By becoming a Friend of Copper Canyon Press you can secure the future – and the legacy – of one of the finest independent publishers in America.

For information and catalogs

COPPER CANYON PRESS
Post Office Box 271
Port Townsend, Washington 98368
360 / 385-4925
coppercanyon@olympus.net
www.ccpress.org

Colophon

The text is set in New Caledonia, a digital version of type designed by W.A. Dwiggins for Linotype in 1939 after the Scotch faces of the nineteenth century. The titles are set in Nofret, designed by calligrapher Gudrun Zapf-von Hesse for Berthold in 1987. Cover art by Laura Popenoe. Book design and composition by Valerie Brewster, Scribe Typography. Printed on archival quality Glatfelter Author's Text (acid-free, recycled stock) at McNaughton & Gunn.